abc BRITISH AIRPORTS

5th Edition

Alan J. Wright

IAN ALLAN
Publishing

CONTENTS

Introduction	3
Abbreviations	5
Aberdeen (Dyce)	7
Belfast International (Aldergrove)	8
Belfast City (Harbour/Sydenham)	10
Bembridge (Isle of Wight)	12
Birmingham (Elmdon)	13
Blackpool (Squires Gate)	16
Bournemouth (Hurn)	17
Bristol (Lulsgate)	20
Cambridge (Teversham)	22
Cardiff International (Rhoose)	24
Carlisle (Crosby)	26
Coventry (Baginton)	28
Dundee (Riverside)	30
East Midlands (Castle Donington)	32
Edinburgh (Turnhouse)	35
Exeter (Clyst Honiton)	36
Gatwick	38
Glasgow (Abbotsinch)	41
Gloucestershire (Staverton)	43
Guernsey	44
Heathrow	46
Humberside (Kirmington)	49
Inverness (Dalcross)	51
Ipswich	52
Isle of Man (Ronaldsway)	54
Jersey	55
Kent International (Manston)	57
Land's End (St Just)	59
Leeds/Bradford (Yeadon)	62
Liverpool (Speke)	65
London City	67
Luton	69
Lydd	72
Manchester (Ringway)	74
Newcastle (Woolsington)	77
Newquay (St Mawgan)	78
Norwich (Horsham St Faith)	80
Penzance	82
Plymouth City	83
Prestwick	85
Scilly Isles (St Mary's)	87
Sheffield	88
Shoreham	88
Southampton (Eastleigh)	90
Southend (Rochford)	93
Stansted	96
Teesside (Middleton St George)	99
Wick	101
Airfields Guide	105

First published 1979
Fifth edition 1996

ISBN 0 7110 2452 9

Published by Ian Allan Publishing

an imprint of Ian Allan Ltd,
Terminal House, Station Approach,
Shepperton, Surrey TW17 8AS.
Printed by Ian Allan Printing Ltd,
Coombelands House, Coombelands Lane,
Addlestone, Surrey KT15 1HY.

Front cover:
Virgin Atlantic's Boeing 747 G-VLAX loading at one of Gatwick's satellite Stands. *Aviation Picture Library*

Title page:
There are no viewing facilities at Glasgow, this shot of the Loganair/British Airways Short SD3-60 being taken from one of the few airside vantage points. *Jean Wright*

Back cover:
Fokker 70s operate into London City. *Fokker*

ACKNOWLEDGEMENTS

Grateful thanks are extended to BAA PLC, the Directors and staff of the many independent airports, the Civil Aviation Authority and the patient and helpful bus enquiry office staff around the country. Of the many individuals who have helped in some way, special thanks must go to George Pennick, Allan S. Wright and Colin Wright.

INTRODUCTION

It has taken many years for air travel to be accepted as an essential mode of transport in the UK. Business travellers now find it possible to visit distant parts and return in one day, thereby reducing time away from the office and eliminating expensive overnight costs. It could be thought that with the ever-advancing electronic technology it should be possible to use computer networks, fax and other devices to replace the need for personal visits. No doubt this is a development not to be encouraged by the airline industry! Inclusive tour charters are used by another large section of the population and it is interesting to note that they now, quite rightly, accept flying as nothing very special.

Facilities at airports have greatly improved in sympathy with the increased patronage and can even provide a good measure of entertainment. Students of human behaviour can find it absorbing to observe the various antics of those in charge of luggage trolleys as the latter resist all attempts to maintain a straight course, especially when negotiating a series of downward slopes. Matching arriving passengers with the multitude of hastily written notices intended to attract the attention of a particular Smith, Garibaldi or Pyng Pong, can also help to while away the time, but the real purpose of the airport should not be forgotten.

Once airside, travellers have the benefit of shops, ranging from a newspaper kiosk at a small unit to a collection of retail outlets at others that would do justice to a large city. However, before reaching this area, security checks are enforced. These are usually conducted without fuss and are an essential, if unfortunate, part of modern society. Nowadays, punctuality has greatly improved with aircraft movements being handled swiftly for quick turnrounds. Boarding is often carried out through airbridges, which seldom gives the passenger a chance to count the number of engines or check the identity of the machine.

Elsewhere on the site, chainlink fences have long been commonplace around perimeters which, while not affecting viewing to any great extent, usually impede photography in some way. It is surprising to note that at Narita, Tokyo's main airport where public protests are legion, holes have been officially provided by the authorities to allow the use of lenses. Unfortunately, those employed to maintain security at UK airports frequently adopt an over-zealous attitude once equipped with a uniform and a small van in which to patrol constantly. Fortunately this is not always the case. Some airports, such as Manchester, Birmingham and Aberdeen, have provided excellent facilities for interested spectators, while others do not actively discourage visitors. Interestingly, a number of military airfields not only provide enclosures at suitable vantage points, but actually offer special opportunities for photography for a small fee. At least it is a means by which to keep the defence budget in funds!

It is hoped that this book will be of use when planning a trip to UK airports. The main section deals with those handling scheduled services with the exception of some of the islands off the British coast, few of which are likely to be frequented by the normal enthusiast! Due note should be taken that the inclusion of a particular operator against an airport does not guarantee the appearance of its aircraft, because all too often airlines disappear without warning. Even ground transportation has become affected by similar practices, causing well-known and long-established bus companies to acquire new names, liveries, route numbers and apparently in many cases, the adoption of minibuses to confuse the occasional traveller. For this reason, no attempt has been made to mention costs because these can regularly change. It is always wise to check that any spectator facilities that are normally available have not been suddenly closed as a result of some international squabble. No one can actually explain the purpose or value of these actions beyond insisting that they are for security reasons, yet such major European airports as Frankfurt, Geneva and Zürich continue to provide excellent facilities, but with visitors searched before entry. This seems a sensible solution for all concerned.

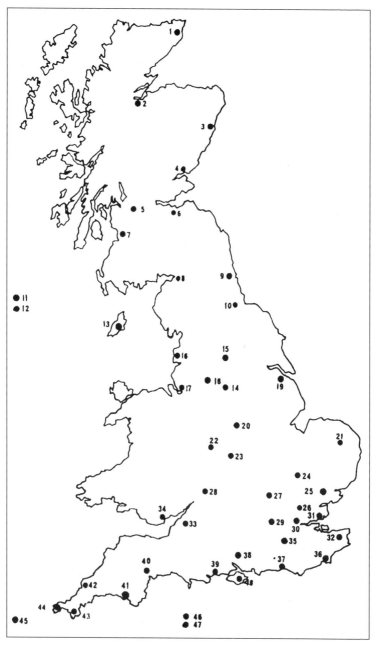

KEY FOR MAP

1	Wick	25	Ipswich
2	Inverness	26	Stansted
3	Aberdeen	27	Luton
4	Dundee	28	Gloucester/Cheltenham
5	Glasgow	29	Heathrow
6	Edinburgh	30	London City
7	Prestwick	31	Southend
8	Carlisle	32	Kent International (Manston)
9	Newcastle	33	Bristol
10	Teesside	34	Cardiff
11	Belfast International (Aldergrove)	35	Gatwick
12	Belfast (City)	36	Lydd
13	Isle of Man	37	Shoreham
14	Sheffield	38	Southampton
15	Leeds/Bradford	39	Bournemouth
16	Blackpool	40	Exeter
17	Liverpool	41	Plymouth
18	Manchester	42	Newquay
19	Humberside	43	Penzance
20	East Midlands	44	Land's End
21	Norwich	45	Isles of Scilly
22	Birmingham	46	Guernsey
23	Coventry	47	Jersey
24	Cambridge	48	Bembridge (Isle of Wight)

ABBREVIATIONS

A/G	Air-ground communication station	FAA	Fleet Air Arm
AAC	Army Air Corps	FIDO	Fog, Intensive Dispersal of
ABC	Air Bridge Carriers		(also known as Fog Investigation
AEF	Air Experience Flight		& Dispersal Operation)
APP	Approach	Flt	Flight
ARRS	Airborne Rescue and	FSS	Flying Selection School
	Recovery Squadron	FTS	Flying Training School
A&AEE	Aircraft and Armament	IT	Inclusive tour
	Experimental Establishment	IWM	Imperial War Museum
BA	British Airways	JAT	Jugoslovenski Aerotransport
BAF	British Air Ferries	KIA	Kent International Airport
BEA	British European Airways	KLM	Royal Dutch Airlines
	& Birmingham European	LOT	Polskie Linie Lotnicze
BIA	British Independent Airways	MCA	Ministry of Civil Aviation
BOAC	British Overseas Airways Corporation	MHz	Megahertz
BR	British Rail	MoD	Ministry of Defence
BWA	British World Airlines	MU	Maintenance Unit
CAA	Civil Aviation Authority	OCU	Operational Conversion Unit
CAF	Canadian Armed Forces	OTU	Operational Training Unit
CFS	Central Flying School	PR	Photo Reconnaissance (Unit)
CTA	Compagnie de Transport Aérien	RAE	Royal Aircraft Establishment
DAT	Delta Air Transport	RCAF	Royal Canadian Air Force
EFTS	Elementary Flying Training School	Reg	Region
E&RFTS	Elementary and Reserve	RFG	Regionalflug
	Flying Training School	RFS	Reserve Flying School

RLG	Relief Landing Ground	TEA	Trans European Airways
SAR	Search and Rescue	TWR	Tower
SAS	Scandinavian Airlines System	TWU	Tactical Weapons Unit
STOL	Short take-off and landing	TWCU	Tactical Weapons Conversion Unit
TAP	Transportes Aereos Portugueses Air Portugal	UAS	University Air Squadron
TAT	Transport Aérien Transrégional	USAAF	United States of America Air Force

Top:
The observation gallery at Belfast International is to the right of the Air Belfast One-Eleven G-AVMN. *AJW*

Above:
Palmair Flightline operates its BAe 146 G-BPNT from Bournemouth. *A. S. Wright*

ABERDEEN (DYCE)

Passenger services were started at Dyce in 1934 when Aberdeen Airways opened a route to Glasgow using a Short Scion and de Havilland Dragon. The following year a service to Edinburgh provided the opportunity to connect with the London flights of North Eastern Airways. The airline later became known as Allied Airways, by which time extensions to the route network took in the northern islands in addition to Wick and Inverness.

The RAF was in evidence at Dyce by 1937 when No 612 Squadron was formed. Initially it was equipped with Hawker Hinds but it was not long before Avro Ansons were on strength. The airfield was requisitioned in 1939, whereupon hard runways were laid for the use of Coastal Command squadrons. Dyce also saw a little civil flying during the war when it was used as the UK terminal for some of the transport services to Sweden.

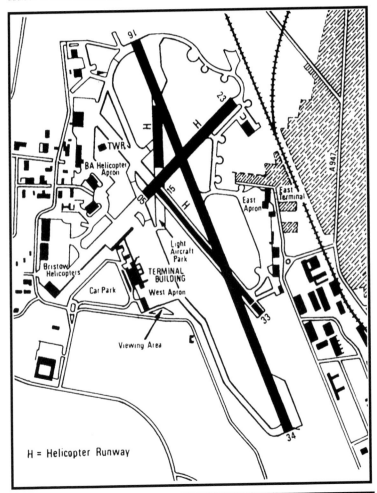

H = Helicopter Runway

7

After the war civil flying was resumed alongside that of the military, scheduled services being undertaken once again by Allied Airways until in 1947 the operations came under the control of BEA.

Expansion was slow with services few until the North Sea oil activity began to have effect. It soon became the fastest growing UK airport, passing to British Airports Authority control on 1 January 1975. Plans were rapidly put into effect to greatly enlarge the facilities, which resulted in a new terminal building, taxiways and apron areas being constructed for a 1977 opening.

Aberdeen also became one of the world's most active bases for helicopters engaged in oil support work. Charter operators were also kept busy, the carriers changing as the contracts came up for review. British Airways uses a mixture of Boeing 757s and Airbus A320s on the lucrative Heathrow route, while the flag carrier continues the Gatwick services acquired from Dan-Air using Boeing 737s. The number of destinations available for travellers has steadily increased, several routes being flown by foreign operators. However, in the mid-1980s a decline in the offshore gas and oil industry became apparent, which in turn brought about a reduction in the number of charter operators active at Aberdeen. Nevertheless, the airport still handles a considerable number of movements.

Location and access: Situated 7 miles northwest of Aberdeen on the A96 from which it is signposted. Charges graduated at both the main and heliport car parks. Bus route 27 runs between the airport terminal and Aberdeen bus/rail station at 40min intervals, less frequently on Sundays. These also call at the heliports every day except Sunday. Journey time is 30min. It is necessary to produce the exact fare on boarding. The east terminal, reached via the A947, is used by some helicopter operators

Terminal: Main building is a modern structure containing Aerogrill, bar, buffet, shop and waiting area
Spectator facilities: None are provided in the terminal. There is a viewing area situated to the south of the building from where it is somewhat poorly signposted. It is necessary to walk along the front of the complex past the cargo sheds until a set of concrete steps are found. Once at the top, a path is followed to the spectators' area. Admission is free. The spot is an excellent, but frequently chilly, vantage point for viewing activity on the apron and runway. Photography is possible through the substantial 10ft fence; a notice proclaims the authority's regret at having been forced to install this standard obstruction
Operators: Scheduled services by Air UK (BAe 146, Fokker 50, Friendship), British Airways (Airbus A320, BAe ATP, Boeing 737/757), Brymon Airways (Dash Seven, Dash Eight), Business Air (SAAB SF340), easyJet (Boeing 737), Gill Airways (ATR42, Short SD3-30/SD3-60), Manx Airlines (Jetstream 31/41), SAS (DC-9, Fokker 50). *Charter and IT operators:* Air Europa (Boeing 737), Air Malta (Boeing 737), British World Airlines (ATR72), Brymon Airways (Dash Seven, Dash Eight), Futura (Boeing 737), Spanair (MD83), Viva Air (Boeing 737). *Helicopter flights:* British International, Bond, Brintel, Bristow. *Cargo/mail flights:* Atlantic Air Transport (Electra), DHL (Convair 580), Flightline (Bandeirante)
Movements (1994): Total 103,056 (air transport 79,984/club 8,112/test & training 8,123/positioning 4,132). Total passengers 2,185,582
Runways: 16/34 (6,000ft/1,820m). 01, 05/23 and 15/33 used only by helicopters
Radio frequencies: 118.1MHz (Tower)/120.4MHz (Approach)/121.25MHz, 128.3MHz (Radar)
Telephone: Aberdeen (01224) 722331
Operated by: Aberdeen Airport Ltd

BELFAST INTERNATIONAL (ALDERGROVE)

The airfield was first used in 1918 although it was not developed until the outbreak of World War 2. During this time it had become the home of No 502 (Ulster) Squadron, which operated initially as a night bomber unit, converting after 10 years to a day bombing role before, in 1938, it took on reconnaissance duties with Coastal Command. Throughout the war various squadrons spent time at Aldergrove to engage either in patrols over the Atlantic or

anti-submarine duties. These operational units were joined by No 23 Maintenance Unit late in 1939, which thereafter handled such types as the Wellington, Hampden and Blenheim. The airfield was also chosen to receive the first deliveries of the American-built Hudson, the pioneering seven flying across from Newfoundland. After the war regular Met flights were flown by No 202 Squadron equipped initially with Halifaxes, this type being replaced with the more modern Hastings in 1950. It was an essential duty which was to last until mid-1964. During this period the Ulster auxiliary squadron was in residence equipped with the Mosquito, Spitfire and lastly the Vampire, before the unit was forced to disband in 1957.

Until 1963 the airlines had used Nutts Corner for their Belfast operations, but space on the site was so limited that expansion was not practical. On 26 September all services were moved to Aldergrove which had been rebuilt as Northern Ireland's gateway. When it was opened the airport possessed a brand-new modern terminal complex incorporating the now familiar pier loading system. It has since been developed to enable it to handle transatlantic movements, although for many years this traffic tended to use Prestwick, passengers being ferried across the water by connecting feeder flights. This practice has now ceased with North American ITs originating at Aldergrove, although the airport still has no schedules on this route, other than Aer Lingus thrice-weekly flights via Shannon.

Over the past five years, Belfast International has invested some £25 million, with the assistance of the European Regional Development fund, into the facility. Major projects have included the East Terminal extension which incorporated the renovation of the airline passenger lounges, modernisation of the domestic baggage reclaim, relocation of the information centre and the provision of extra seating in the Departure Concourse. Now over 30 years old, the spacious building compares very favourably with much younger structures.

Like the two principal Scottish cities, Belfast has a shuttle service to London flown by British Airways. With the retirement of the Trident in December 1985, the trunk route was taken over by Boeing 757s, but flights are now operated by the smaller 737. Competition on this route is supplied by British Midland's 737s, while until 1991 Dan-Air offered an alternative London terminal by using Gatwick for its One-Elevens and 146s. Air Belfast was due to restart the route with One-Elevens towards the end of 1995, but the operation was suspended after a few flights over the Christmas period. On the debit side, Aldergrove lost some of its commuter traffic to Belfast Harbour from February 1983, the latter being situated much nearer to the city centre.

Any deficiencies in total traffic are expected to be restored by the increased amount of freight handled by the airport. At the beginning of 1991 a new £7 million cargo complex with its own dedicated terminal and associated offices opened. An apron extension was

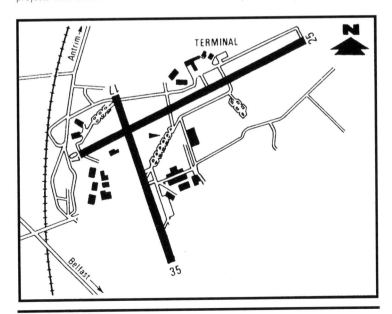

included in the development to accommodate the latest Boeing 747-400 freighters.

Currently the unit handles about 35,000 tonnes of cargo per annum and is the second largest regional centre in the UK. Large consignments of goods from Northern Ireland's textile and electronic industries already provide regular loads for shipment to mainland UK, a business likely to grow with the improving economic situation.

The number of passenger services has greatly increased following the peace initiative, with new links to a number of destinations, more capacity on the flights together with improved frequencies. A revival of the tourist industry in particular should bring welcome income to the airport and the Province in general.

Location and access: Situated 13 miles northwest of Belfast on A26, 4 miles south of Antrim. Car park charges graduated. Buses run half-hourly from Great Victoria Street bus station to the airport with a journey time of 40min
Terminal: Contains bar, restaurant, self-service buffet, shops and lounge area
Spectator facilities: An indoor gallery in front of the first floor departure lounge overlooks the apron allowing all movements to be easily seen. Photography is also possible through the lightly tinted glass. There is no admission charge
Operators: Aer Lingus (Airbus A330), British

Airways (BAe ATP, Boeing 737), British Midland (BAe ATP, Boeing 737, Fokker 70), Business Air (SAAB SF340), Jersey European Airways (BAe 146), KLM (Fokker 70), Loganair (Short SD3-60), Maersk Air (One-Eleven, Boeing 737). *Charter and IT operators:* Air Club International (Airbus A310), Air Europa (Boeing 737), Airtours International (Airbus A320, Boeing 757), Air Transat (TriStar), Airworld (Airbus A320), American Trans Air (Boeing 757, TriStar), Balkan (Tu-154), British Midland (Boeing 737), Deutsche BA (Fokker 100), Futura (Boeing 737), Leisure International (Boeing 767), Monarch (Boeing 757), Royal Airlines (TriStar), Ryanair (Boeing 737), Spanair (MD83). *Cargo/mail flights:* BAC Express (Short SD3-30), British World Airlines (Viscount), Business Air (SAAB SF340), Channel Express (Herald), Emerald Airways (HS 748), Gill Airways (ATR72, Short SD3-60), HeavyLift Cargo Airlines (Belfast), Loganair (Short SD3-60), TNT (BAe 146, Boeing 727)
Movements (1994): Total 88,325 (air transport 32,877/club 3,445/private 9,792/military 36,361/positioning 4,026). Total passengers 2,057,791
Runways: 07/25 (9,111ft/2,777m), 17/35 (6,400ft/1,951m)
Radio frequencies: 118.3MHz (Tower)/120.0MHz (Approach)/120.9MHz (Radar)
Telephone: Antrim (01849) 422888
Operated by: Belfast International Airport Ltd

BELFAST CITY (HARBOUR/SYDENHAM)

When some reclaimed land in Belfast harbour became available, the opportunity was taken by Harland & Wolff to construct a new yard for its shipbuilding activities. Later an aerodrome was built alongside the premises and the company moved into the aircraft business in association with the Rochester-based Short Bros. Although ideally situated, the somewhat soggy nature of the surface was not suitable for commercial operations when it was completed in 1933, but following the erection of a large factory by the owners, new drainage schemes rectified the problem. Officially opened on 16 March 1938 by the Prime Minister's wife, the new site soon attracted airlines away from the other Belfast airport at Newtownards.

Aircraft production started in 1936, with the newly created Short & Harland given the task of building Bristol Bombays, Blenheim sections and the in-line engine version of the Hampden known as the Handley Page Hereford. Shorts had secured the contract to supply the RAF's

first four-engined bomber which was to become known as the Stirling. Production of the new type at Rochester was painfully slow, so to speed matters a new line was installed at Sydenham, with work on the first batch starting in June 1940. It continued until eventually more than half of the 2,381 machines produced had been built at the Northern Ireland site.

By this time the airfield was under the control of the RAF and was used by squadrons employed in the city's defence. From November 1941 the airfield took the name of RAF Belfast, but with an increasing presence by naval squadrons it was inevitable that in June 1943 another change found it with the identity of HMS *Gadwall*. Ideal facilities existed for ease of loading carriers since the airfield was alongside the docks. For this reason the base was also the arrival point of vast numbers of American-built warplanes that were shipped across the Atlantic. Unloaded from the decks of the cargo vessels, the machines were quickly test flown before delivery to the maintenance units on the mainland.

After the war Shorts converted Sunderlands and Seafords into civil transports, while in the 1950s the company became involved in building some of the Britannias for Bristol after the Sydenham runway had been extended to 6,000ft in 1952. Original Short Bros designs were built and flown, the most impressive being the giant Belfast freighter which sadly attracted no orders other than 10 for the RAF. In the 1960s the company's efforts were directed into the Skyvan, later developed into the 30-seat SD3-30 and the larger SD3-60 commuter airliners, both proving very popular with the smaller airlines, particularly in America.

Commercial operations were carried out at Nutts Corner after the war, but, while suitable for the airliners of the day, the larger types coming into service in the late 1950s needed more space, something that the airport could not offer. Accordingly Aldergrove became Belfast's airport in September 1963, providing all the modern facilities demanded by the new equipment and travelling public. However, in 1983 Short Bros was persuaded to reopen its airfield at Belfast/Harbour (as Sydenham was now known) to commercial traffic. Blackpool-based Spacegrand became the first airline to move its Irish terminal, quickly followed by others such as Loganair.

Growth was rapid as travellers came to realise the advantages of its position close to the city centre. At first almost all services used either the SD3-30 or 3-60, although on occasions the Viscount appeared at peak times. Thereafter the number of routes available gradually grew until by 1990 they equalled those offered by Aldergrove. Several, such as Manchester and Leeds, were in competition, the passengers' choice usually depending on whether onward flights were involved. Until mid-June that year, five operators (Manx, Loganair, Jersey European, Gill Air and Capital) shared the traffic using Friendships, SD3-30/3-60s and BAe 748/ATP/146s.

Operators have remained fairly consistent, although Capital and newcomer Genesis fell by the wayside. The latter's route from East Midlands was taken over by Community Express in December 1995, once again using SD3-60s. Jersey European has developed its activities at the airport to provide frequent services to Gatwick and Stansted, together with connections to link Londonderry with the trunk routes. Although the loss of business was not popular with the Aldergrove authorities, the two airports have settled down to share the traffic.

Location and access: Situated directly beside a main dual carriageway 2 miles from the city centre on the east side of Belfast docks. Journey time by road is 5min. Alternatively there is a rail station 100yd from the terminal which is reached by using the footbridge provided.

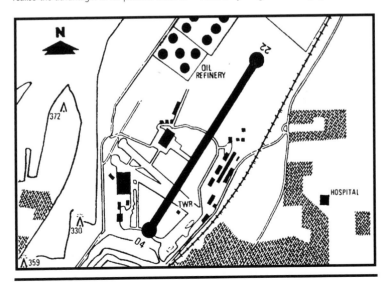

NI Railways operates frequent services to Belfast Central taking only 5min to complete the journey. A Citybus service leaves the station forecourt every 30min on weekdays (40min at weekends) bound for City Hall
Terminal: Contains buffet and bar
Spectator facilities: None provided. Vantage points can be found on the perimeter and car park
Operators: Scheduled services by Community Express (Short SD3-60), Gill Airways (ATR42/72, Short SD3-60), Jersey European Airways (BAe 146, Friendship, Short SD3-60), Manx Airlines (BAe ATP, Jetstream 31/41)
Movements (1994): Total 40,197 (air transport 31,938/military 5,782/private 1,094). Total passengers 1,229,508
Runway: 04/22 (6,000ft/1,829m)
Radio frequencies: 130.75MHz (Tower)/130.85MHz (Approach)/134.8MHz (Radar)
Telephone: Belfast (01232) 457745
Operated by: Belfast City Airport Services Ltd

BEMBRIDGE (ISLE OF WIGHT)

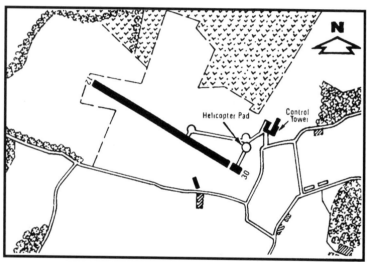

In the early 1920s a landing ground was created on ground belonging to a local farm. For many years it was used by private aircraft visiting the Isle of Wight, but in the mid-1930s Spartan Air Lines operated scheduled services into the airfield, although its merger with United in 1935 brought an end to the venture. At this time there were more popular airfields at Sandown, Ryde and Cowes, each of these being included in various route networks before the war and even into the 1950s.

Nowadays Bembridge is far better known as the home of Pilatus Britten-Norman and the Islander family, but in the 1980s there were several attempts made by carriers to restart regular flights to the island. While these efforts to introduce schedules have so far been unsuccessful, a local tour operator, Bath Travel, operated its first charter flight to Jersey in September 1985 using an Islander for the return trip. The programme was expanded in the two years that followed when the increased number of flights were maintained by a 14-seat Trislander operated by Aurigny Air Services. Due to popular demand, even more capacity was necessary in 1988 and 1989 which was achieved by employing an 18-seat Brymon Twin Otter for the sorties. Finally Bath Travel arranged to charter a Dash Seven from London City for its short season in September 1990, the 44-seat type being the largest commercial airliner capable of using Bembridge. Special Customs services have to be provided since none are normally available at the airfield. Two series of flights were planned for 1991 (spring and autumn) once again using the Dash Seven, but this time in British Midland's livery.

Location and access: Situated alongside the B3395 Brading-Bembridge road, 1 mile southwest of the latter
Terminal: Refreshments can be obtained at the Propeller Inn

Spectator facilities: None provided. Views of all activities are possible from the perimeter
Operators: Surrey & Kent Charter Services (Seneca)
Movements (1994): Total 9,934 (test & training 811/club 2,077/private 5,975)
Runway: 12/30 (2,746ft/837m)
Radio frequency: 123.25MHz (Tower)
Telephone: Bembridge (01983) 872511
Operated by: Pilatus Britten-Norman Ltd

BIRMINGHAM (ELMDON)

Plans to establish a municipal airport were initiated by the City Council as early as February 1928, but another eight years passed before construction began. The distinction of becoming the first aircraft to land on the newly-laid grass went to Western Airways' DH90 Dragonfly registered G-AEDH, but it was on 1 May that the airport opened for business This time it was the Swallow G-ACXE which was the first arrival, having transported the Lord Mayor from nearby Castle Bromwich for the occasion. Later that day the inaugural scheduled service was handled when a Rapide of Great Western and Southern Airlines touched down after its trip from Liverpool to Manchester. Following the customary addresses by the civic authorities, the machine was allowed to resume its journey south to its next stop at Bristol *en route* to Southampton and Ryde. As it left, the assembled guests were given a second chance to indulge in some harmless pomp when the four-engined DH86 G-AEFH arrived. Operated by Railway Air Services, it was on its regular journey to Liverpool and Glasgow.

Nevertheless, some work was still outstanding on the terminal building, while levelling of the 800-acre site continued. Another two months of intensive work completed the initial phase of the undertaking and on 2 July the first foreign commercial movement was recorded when a KLM DC-2 arrived from Schiphol. There were three grass landing strips available, each 3,000ft in length, with a fourth earmarked for use in conditions of bad visibility since it was 900ft longer. Six days later Elmdon was formally opened by the Duchess of Kent and operations began in earnest.

At the beginning of the war No 14 Elementary Flying Training School (EFTS) was established, Tiger Moths thereafter becoming the resident landmarks for over six years as control of the airfield had been assumed by the Air Ministry on 16 September 1939. Not only was Elmdon suitable for flying training, it also became the flight test centre for Stirlings and Lancasters built by Austin Longbridge. Assembled at the Marston Green shadow factory, they were then towed for their aerial

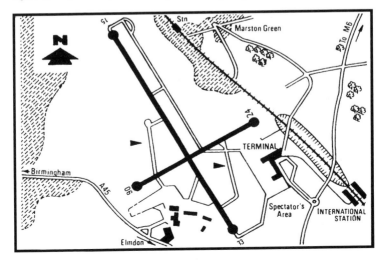

baptism from the short-lived airport. Demob came on 19 June 1946, but instead of reverting to Birmingham Council it became the responsibility of the Ministry of Civil Aviation. For some time flying was restricted to club or charter movements, but after representations to the authorities, BEA eventually launched a scheduled service to Paris in partnership with Air France on 8 April 1949. At last the Midlands had a regular link with the Continent and it was joined shortly after by both Swissair and Aer Lingus operations.

It was not a time of rapid growth for the aviation industry, so notable events were scarce during the airport's early postwar years. However, there was one highlight on 22 December 1954 when a Sabena DC-4 landed after a transatlantic flight, the first such movement for Birmingham. While its arrival did not create any major difficulties, it did serve to illustrate the future trend.

Impatient to regain its long-lost possession, the Council submitted a request to the Ministry once more, but as on previous occasions a firm rejection was received. Undeterred, the city's authorities persevered until finally on 1 April 1960 the battle was won: Birmingham had its airport again after nearly 21 years. As some form of compensation an improvement grant was awarded to provide a much-needed extension to the terminal, which was duly opened by the Duchess of Kent on 28 April 1961.

During its requisitioned time the site had benefited by the provision of two hard runways, one of which had been extended to 5,000ft (1,562m) prior to the handover in 1960. Further lengthening in 1967 took the main strip to 7,400ft (2,255.5m) making it possible for the economic operation of the modern types then entering service. This brought the need for more terminal expansion, a new Customs hall and more space for the bar and buffet. Despite all the work it was not long before there were signs that congestion was returning as the number of passengers passing through steadily increased.

There was no scope for extending the existing terminal yet again, so plans were made to build a brand-new complex elsewhere on the site. After prolonged discussions and inquiries the scheme was authorised, allowing work to commence in April 1981. Designed to cater for three million passengers and 33,000 movements annually by 1990, the new terminal was positioned on the northeast side of the main runway. Ideally it should have been incorporated with Birmingham International

railway station, thereby providing a single integrated unit, but the extensive earthworks and other restrictions ruled the idea out on cost grounds. As a result, a 600m transit system was installed to link the two buildings. It was 4 April 1984 when the long-awaited day arrived and the new facility was ready for business.

First scheduled flight away was the Birmingham Executive Airways Jetstream G-OBEA which left for Zürich followed by G-AVGP, a One-Eleven of British Airways bound for Aberdeen. In accordance with tradition there was an official ceremony at a later date, this time undertaken by The Queen and Prince Philip on 30 May. A plaque recording the event was unveiled in the entrance; the Maglev transit system later received the Royal seal of approval when the couple took a ride to the National Exhibition Centre. Meanwhile, the airport's traffic figures began to reflect the vast improvements as the airlines introduced new services in response to the demand.

Both 1987 and 1988 returned a passenger growth rate of 25% so an £11 million project to provide more accommodation in the terminal was begun. After the opening of the new buildings in 1984, the disused passenger building site had been adopted for freight handling. In view of the steady increase in this business, plans were also made to provide additional facilities starting in 1989.

During the same year, work began in conjunction with British Airways on a £50 million development to provide a specially-designed hub terminal. Located on the extended apron to the east of the domestic pier, the latter was demolished as the new building progressed. When operational 10 airbridge-equipped stands became available for the exclusive use of BA and initially Birmingham European.

After its relaunch at the beginning of 1989, BEA became a major force at the airport. It steadily increased the scope of its European network, at the same time introducing jets on the routes previously flown by Gulfstreams and Jetstreams. Birmingham became a hub for the airline's Belfast and Newcastle services which were timed to connect with the European flights. At last there was a realisation that a convenient alternative to Heathrow and Gatwick was available, a fact confirmed by the impressive passenger figures achieved. In May 1992 BEA was merged with Brymon Airways, the other member of the TPL Group, whereupon the combined force took the title Brymon European Airways. Birmingham remained one of the carrier's main centres with the same network of schedules continued by the same aircraft, but the arrangement was short-lived. Following the dissolution of the loss-making TPL Group, Brymon and Birmingham European once again became separate entities, the latter being sold to the Danish company, Maersk Air, which began operations as a BA franchise holder on 1 August 1993. Brymon on the other hand, became a full subsidiary of the flag carrier with its aircraft carrying the latter's full livery.

In addition to the scheduled traffic, Birmingham also handles a considerable number of IT flights which are operated by a variety of carriers. At one point in 1989, the airport became the base for TEA UK, a new company set up by the management of Orion Airways after the latter was taken over by Britannia. However, following the failure of its Belgian parent company, it was forced to cease operations after a relatively short career. More recently, Community Express established itself at the airport in 1995 prior to launching services to Gatwick and East Midlands.

Location and access: Situated 6 miles east-southeast of Birmingham on north side of A45. M6 Junction 4 and M42 Junction 6 provide easy access. A West Midlands bus route connects the airport with the city centre and Coventry, while another serves the needs of those wishing to travel to Walsall and Wolverhampton. There are also other local services available. National Express provides a number of routes to various destinations in East Anglia, the southwest and the northeast. A coach calls at the airport on its regular visits to similar locations at Manchester, Luton, Heathrow and Gatwick. There are frequent trains on both local and InterCity services taking 10min from Birmingham (New Street) and 80min from London (Euston). It takes only 90sec to travel by the Maglev transporter from station to terminal. Multi-storey car parks for short-term use are situated adjacent to the terminal, while ample open areas are available for longer stays or visitors. Charges vary according to which is used and the duration

Terminal: Contains good refreshment facilities, bar and shops

Spectator facilities: A glass-fronted covered terrace is provided on the upper floor of the terminal overlooking the apron. There is a small charge. Photography is possible with care. A large opened grassed area alongside the southern taxiway affords an excellent vantage point for viewing. Due to the need for additional land for the Eurohub, some of the

space allocated for spectators was absorbed for the new structure. This in turn necessitated the resiting of the security fence so that it now comprises the normal form of obstruction for photographers. Nevertheless, with care it is still possible to obtain shots through the chainlink barrier. In any case the shadow caused by the wire disappears if using a 200mm lens. There is no charge made for entry. The authorities are to be congratulated for recognising the need for such a facility and ensuring that it has been retained despite the terminal expansion

Operators: Scheduled services by Aer Lingus (BAe 146, Fokker 50), Air France (Boeing 737), Air Malta (Airbus A320, Boeing 737), Air 2000 (Boeing 757), American Airlines (Boeing 767), BASE Regional Airlines (Jetstream 31), British Airways (BAe ATP, Boeing 737/757), British Midland (BAe ATP, Fokker 70), Community Express (Jetstream 31, Short SD3-60), Crossair (RJ85, SAAB 2000), Cyprus Airways (Airbus A310/A320), Jersey European Airways (BAe 146, Friendship), KLM CityHopper (Fokker 50/70, SAAB SF340), Lufthansa (Airbus A320, Boeing 737, Canadair RJ, Fokker 50), Maersk Air (One-Eleven, Boeing 737, Jetstream 31), Manx Airlines (BAe ATP, Jetstream 41), Newair (Jetstream 31), Ryanair (Boeing 737), Tajik Air (Airbus A310), Turkmenistan (Boeing 737).
Charter and IT operators: Air Europa (Boeing 737), Air Malta (Boeing 737), Airtours International (Airbus A320, Boeing 757), Air Transat (Boeing 757, TriStar), Air VIA (Tu-154), Air 2000 (Boeing 757), British Airways (BAe ATP, Boeing 737/757), Britannia Airways (Boeing 757/767), British World Airlines (BAe 146, One-Eleven), Canada 3000 (Boeing 757), Centennial (MD83), Cyprus Airways (Airbus A310), Eurocypria (Airbus A320), Futura (Boeing 737), GB Airways (Boeing 737), Leisure International (Airbus A320, Boeing 767), Manx Airlines (BAe 146), Maersk Air (Boeing 737, One-Eleven), Monarch Airlines (Airbus A320, Boeing 757), Royal Air Maroc (Boeing 737), Sabre Airways (Boeing 737), Spanair (MD83), Sunway (MD83), Viva Air (Boeing 737)

Movements (1994): Total 95,278 (air transport 71,068/club 11,132/private 8,012). Total passengers 4,943,189

Runways: 15/33 (7,398ft/2,255m), 06/24 (4,314ft/1,315m)

Radio frequencies: 118.3MHz (Tower)/118.05MHz/131.325MHz, (Radar)

Telephone: Birmingham (0121) 767 5511 (switchboard)/(0121) 767 7145 (information)

Operated by: Birmingham International Airport plc.

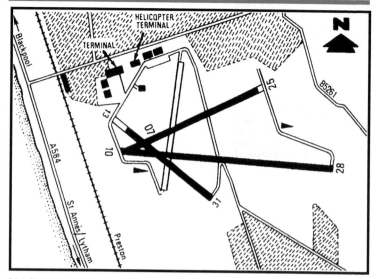

BLACKPOOL (SQUIRES GATE)

The site of the present airport was the scene, in October 1909, of the first flying display to be held in Britain. Scheduled passenger services were started by Blackpool and West Coast Air Service in 1933 when a couple of routes were opened to Liverpool and the Isle of Man using a Fox Moth and a Dragon. These scheduled operations were transferred to nearby Stanley Park in 1937, leaving Squires Gate a quieter place until the outbreak of war.

Due to its position, the airfield was selected by the Air Ministry for development into a standard RAF station with three runways in triangular formation. It was handed over in December 1940 and although various units had lodged at the airfield during the reconstruction period, the first permanent resident was No 3 School of General Reconnaissance equipped with Bothas and later Ansons. The unit was not alone, since various fighter squadrons involved in the defence of the northern cities were also based at Squires Gate from time to time. The occasional visit by a diverted Railway Air Services Rapide also added to the variety.

In addition to its operational and training role, the airfield was chosen as the site for a large shadow factory for the Ministry of Aircraft Production. Blackpool subsequently played a big part in the production of the many Wellington variants, especially after the

bombing of the parent factory at Weybridge.

After the war, training quickly terminated with the station passing to care and maintenance on 10 October 1945. The MCA assumed control in 1946, whereupon charter and air-taxi work was started, particularly by Lancashire Aircraft Corporation. Later this company became one of the airlines permitted to operate scheduled services from Blackpool to such places as Leeds, London, Jersey, Southport and the ever popular Isle of Man. By the mid-1960s international routes had been added, the airlines involved being British United (CI) Airways, Aer Lingus, Autair and Starways. This situation did not last, however, with eventually only British Island Airways left to provide scheduled services to Belfast, Dublin, Isle of Man, Jersey and Rotterdam via Manchester. Air UK inherited such a network when the airline assumed responsibility in January 1980, but it was not long before only Jersey and the Isle of Man routes remained active. Some of the licences were taken up in 1981 by a newcomer to the scheduled scene, Spacegrand operating Navajos to Dublin and Belfast. Loganair also introduced a seasonal Belfast sector into its network employing a Short SD3-30 for the purpose. Air UK wound up its Herald maintenance base at Blackpool, transferring the work to Norwich. The facility was taken over by

Air Atlantique which for a time based several of its DC-3 fleet at the airport. This type of aircraft was no stranger to Blackpool, since much of the TV series *Airline* was filmed locally.

Another significant change came in late 1982, when Manx Airlines took over the responsibility for the Isle of Man services. This new company was set up as a joint venture by Air UK and British Midland, each contributing aircraft from its fleet. Further reorganisation found Spacegrand under the same ownership as Jersey European in the mid-1980s. Gradually resources were combined until the former name disappeared, leaving JEA to operate the northern network from Blackpool. The airport has also become the base for helicopters supporting the oil industry in the Irish Sea, resulting in a new terminal being provided exclusively for this traffic.

A considerable number of movements are generated by the local charter and air-taxi companies in addition to the club and private aircraft based at the airport. On occasions commercial diversions are handled, especially when some unexpected strike closes Manchester. A new terminal was opened in 1995 having been built on land alongside its predecessor.

Location and access: Situated 2.5 miles south of Blackpool off the A584 and about 3 miles from the end of the M55 motorway. Daily rate for car parking. A Blackpool Transport service runs frequently to the bus station with a journey time of about 15min. It is also but a short walk from the seafront tram terminus to the airport entrance.

Terminal: A modern single-storey building was opened in 1995. It offers a lounge area, buffet and bar and occupies the ground previously used as a spectators' viewing area

Spectator facilities: None specifically provided, but vantage points can be found in the terminal area. An alternative spot can be found on the southern perimeter, from where movements on Runway 10/28 can be photographed using a 200mm lens

Operators: Scheduled services by Jersey European Airways (BAe 146, Friendship, Short SD3-60), Manx Airlines (BAe ATP). *Charter and IT operators:* Brymon Airways (Dash Eight), Ryanair (Boeing 737)

Movements (1994): Total 45,877 (air transport 6,241/club 21,570/private 15,971/positioning/806). Total passengers 80,397

Runways: 10/28 (6,132ft/1,869m), 07/25 (2,854ft/870m), 13/31 (3,524ft/1,074m)

Radio frequencies: 118.4MHz (Tower)/135.95MHz (Approach)/119.95MHz (Radar)

Telephone: Blackpool (01253) 343434

Operated by: Blackpool Airport Ltd

BOURNEMOUTH (HURN)

The airfield was opened for the RAF on 1 August 1941. Initially the home of the Telecommunications Flying Unit, Hurn was soon brought into use as the UK terminal for long-range transport flights by Liberators. In May 1942 the TFU departed, making way for the Whitleys of Nos 296 and 297 Squadrons. The two units were thereafter engaged in intensive paratroop training exercises, later in the year extending their activities to include glider towing.

The USAAF took over in November for the duration of an exercise. As a temporary measure the RAF moved out, No 296 Squadron returning alone just before Christmas 1942. Almost immediately the Whitleys began to be replaced by Albemarles, the type making its first operational sorties from Hurn. While detached to North Africa, the squadron's place was taken by No 295 Squadron, again in the process of discarding Whitleys in favour of Albemarles. The return of No 296 at the end of 1943 meant that there were three Albemarle units at Hurn since in the meantime No 570 Squadron had been formed.

The airfield was transferred to Fighter Command in March 1944, the troop carriers moving to other bases in readiness for the invasion of Europe. Hurn began a period of intense activity, various fighter squadrons using it for short periods. On 4 August once again the airfield passed to the Americans, this time for the B-26 Marauders of the 397th Bomb Group. It was another short stay, almost marking the end of military occupation of Hurn. The RAF handed the responsibility for the airfield to the Ministry of Civil Aviation on 31 October 1944.

From this date until 1 June 1946, BOAC operated various services from Hurn before transferring its activities to Heathrow and Northolt. The move of the airlines, which included KLM and Sabena, to the new London Airport meant that activity was much reduced. However, by the early 1950s Vickers-Armstrongs

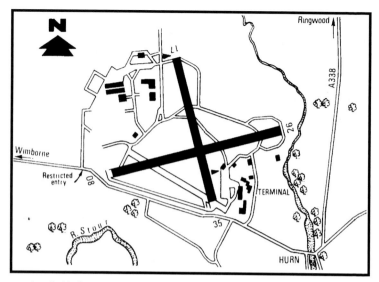

were installed in factory accommodation to produce such types as the Varsity, Viscount and much later, the One-Eleven.

Scheduled services were reintroduced in the early 1950s with Jersey Airlines becoming the major carrier in those days. Other airlines launched themselves into the business only to fail one by one. Silver City brought its car ferry operation to Hurn, mainly as a result of the unsatisfactory conditions at Southampton. Both Cambrian and BEA were also active at Hurn at this time for similar reasons, but on completion of the improvements at Eastleigh, they resumed their earlier routes.

In 1967 Channel was forced to vacate Portsmouth, turning to Bournemouth as an alternative centre for its Jersey service. This was later inherited by Dan-Air, Hurn also becoming the southern terminal for one of its Link City sectors, although in 1982 this part of the airline's network was transferred to Metropolitan Airways using Twin Otters for the purpose. Sadly the carrier was forced to cease operations in August 1985 by which time Short SD3-30s were replacing the original equipment. Dan-Air continued to provide daily flights to the Channel Islands boosted by extra sorties at weekends, but for the 1987 season the company greatly reduced its operations from Bournemouth, limiting its services to Jersey only on Saturdays and Sundays. This move resulted from the CAA's award of licences to

Jersey European which enabled it to start daily flights to the two larger islands early in January. During 1986 Air Camelot provided links with Cherbourg, Bristol and Alderney using Islanders and Trislanders, but these were withdrawn with the demise of the company. Soon afterwards Regency Airways intimated its interest in a similar network, but no services were forthcoming. Early in 1988 newcomer Air Metro announced its plans to fly schedules (subject to CAA approval) on Paris and Amsterdam routes with a target date in June.

This passed without any signs of commercial movements, although the company's new Metro was exhibited at the September Farnborough show. It was destined to be the nearest that the aircraft got to potential passengers because its would-be operator was taken over by Ellan-Vannin before any services were offered. The new owner was not convinced by the type's suitability for the sectors envisaged, so it was announced that Jetstreams would be substituted. Start-up was planned for the spring of 1989 with the proposed routes remaining largely unchanged apart from the addition of a link with Manchester. At least Bournemouth gained one new schedule this time because the service when launched intended using a Navajo for the thrice daily return. Despite all the confident publicity, EVA failed in its bid to introduce European sectors to Amsterdam, Paris and

Brussels and after a year even the single domestic service was discontinued. Guernsey-based Air Sarnia bought the airline in the summer of 1990, but within a few weeks this carrier was also forced to cease trading.

All hope was not lost because a new company known as Southern Airways was already actively preparing itself to enter the scheduled scene. The familiar destinations across the Channel were earmarked but the first venture was planned to be a link with Glasgow using a SAAB SF340. Needless to say, the carrier never reached an operational status, leaving the 5.5 million inhabitants of Bournemouth's catchment area with the prospect of Gatwick or Heathrow. More hopes were raised in early 1994, when newcomer Euro Direct announced ambitious plans for a series of regional services using Bournemouth as its first hub. After all the non-events, it was treated with caution at first, but unlike all the others, this time the scheme came to fruition. After much hard work, Euro Direct operated its first commercial flights in early April, offering both domestic and international schedules. Rapid expansion followed, with new sectors and hubs being added almost weekly. Then came the decline as uneconomic routes were axed, with Bournemouth's operations amongst those affected. After a general review of its affairs, the airline eventually decided to cease trading in mid-February 1995, bringing an end to a brief but enterprising career. It also left Bournemouth deprived of its scheduled services. Locally based Channel Express is also familiar with the islands because it flies regular sorties to and from Jersey and Guernsey with freight using both its Herald and Electra fleets. These movements plus the growing number of IT charters available have helped the airport's economy considerably. Fortunately its developing neighbour at Southampton does not want to attract large-scale IT traffic so Bournemouth should continue to benefit in this case.

Location and access: Situated 4 miles northeast of the Bournemouth/Christchurch/Poole conurbation. The airport is well signposted off the A338 which joins the main A31/M27 some 7 miles inland. Car park fees are graduated and charged on a pay-and-display basis. Buses pass the access road on their way to and from Christchurch but are infrequent

Terminal: The attractive and well-appointed building contains a lounge, cafeteria, bar and shop, the latter offering a good selection of aviation books

Spectator facilities: There is an entrance-free terrace along the front of the buildings which overlooks the apron to provide a good position for viewing and photography, particularly in the morning and early afternoon. It is made possible because of the commendable decision to create a deep grass covered ditch between the public and the restricted area, into which was built the usual high security fence. The result maintains the intended function of the barrier, but allows unobstructed viewing over the top. Full marks for originality. There are also good vantage points along the road bordering the southern perimeter with excellent photographic possibilities, but there is no parking along this section

Operators: Scheduled services suspended. *Charter and IT operators:* Air Europa (Boeing 737), Aurigny Air Services (Short SD3-60, Trislander), Palmair Flightline (BAe 146), Spanair (MD83), South Coast Airways (DC-3), Titan Airways (ATR42). *Freight flights:* Channel Express (Electra, Friendship, Herald). There are numerous movements by school, club, company and privately owned aircraft, both UK and foreign registered. Notable amongst these are the Falcons of FR Aviation and the warbird types of Jet Heritage

Movements (1994): 90,025 (air transport 8,467/positioning 1,635/club 52,371/private 16,688/military 10,788). Total passengers 118,411

Runways: 08/26 (6,030ft/1,838m), 17/35 (4,483ft/1,476m). There is space within the airport boundary to extend 08/26 a further 1,155ft/350m when required

Radio frequencies: 125.6MHz (Tower)/119.625MHz (Approach)

Telephone: Bournemouth (01202) 593939

Operated by: Bournemouth International Airport plc

BRISTOL (LULSGATE)

Broadfield Down was the name allocated to this Air Ministry station, but this was dropped in favour of Lulsgate Bottom. Built in 1939, its planned purpose was to serve as a nightfighter base, but in the event it proved unsatisfactory for this role. Instead a Tiger Moth EFTS moved in on completion, remaining until the airfield was temporarily closed to allow the construction of hard runways. Thereafter Oxfords and Masters were employed on training work throughout the war.

For some years after the departure of the RAF, gliders were the sole users of the airfield. However, it was selected to become the new Bristol airport in the fifties, officially being opened on 1 May 1957 after a new terminal block had been provided. The first scheduled service was in fact flown by a Cambrian Heron on 15 April after transferring the operation from Whitchurch.

This airline accounted for most of the scheduled traffic at Lulsgate in the early days, so it followed that when the general slump of 1958 seriously affected Cambrian, the airport was equally involved. Although the carrier began a slow growth the following year, as a precaution the Lulsgate authorities also invited Dan-Air to serve the area. This operator started both domestic and international services from Bristol in 1960, some of the routes flown surviving to the present day. The third airline quickly on the scene was Aer Lingus with a Dublin service, followed in 1962 by a link with the new airport at Cork.

Throughout the 1970s, Cambrian and later its successor, British Airways, served Lulsgate with Viscounts and One-Elevens on a variety of routes including the Channel Islands, Paris and Belfast. However, these were steadily cut back in frequency until, in 1980, the carrier terminated its association with the airport. Its departure left all services in the hands of Aer Lingus and Dan-Air, the latter picking up some of the licences recently vacated. One significant change to come later was the successful application by the airline to compete with the Irish carrier on the Dublin run. However, the traffic failed to justify two carriers, in due course leaving Aer Lingus to maintain the route alone once again. In an effort to improve the situation Short SD3-60s replaced the One-Elevens on the services which at the same time were increased in frequency. The most significant addition to the Bristol schedules was the introduction of links with Paris, Amsterdam and Düsseldorf

flown by Air France, NetherLines and DLT respectively during 1986 and 1987, although the German carrier subsequently dropped the route.

At the time, however, this type of business only accounted for some 28% of the Bristol traffic, the other 72% coming from the flourishing IT market. All the major tour operators include the airport in their programmes using a mixture of UK and foreign carriers. As the demand increased so there was scope for a new locally-based airline to be formed during 1987. Paramount Airlines subsequently became the first company to use British-registered MD-83s for IT work. To cope with all the extra traffic, a terminal extension phased over six years was begun in the 1980s with the modernisation work in the public areas completed in 1988.

In the meantime the authorities continued the search for carriers interested in starting new scheduled services at Bristol. An encouraging degree of success was achieved with Jersey European adding Belfast City, Jersey, Guernsey and Manchester routes, while Capital offered Leeds and Glasgow, and Aer Lingus extended its Dublin service on to Brussels, at the same time replacing the SD3-60 with Fokker 50s. Sabena also added the Belgian capital to its itinerary at the start of the 1990/91 winter season, in this case contracting the flights to its subsidiary, Delta Air Transport. Bristol had at last acquired a useful batch of destinations with which to attract travellers accustomed to the two-hour trek to Heathrow. There was even more choice available in November 1990 when the airport became the hub for Brymon's new network of routes which included Dublin, Glasgow, Edinburgh and Paris. A further boost was received in March 1991 when Crossair inaugurated a link with Zürich, but despite the early confidence shown by the carrier, the service generated insufficient support and was dropped after a year. There were various other alterations to Bristol's network as uneconomic sectors were pruned from and others added to the coverage, but the destinations available have remained largely unchanged for some time. In 1995 Isles of Scilly Skybus introduced its Twin Otter to links with Newquay, Exeter and the Scillies, sectors that Brymon plied some years earlier, while towards the end of the year, the latter was joined on the Paris route by Brit Air. This growth of the scheduled market came at a fortunate time, because in the late

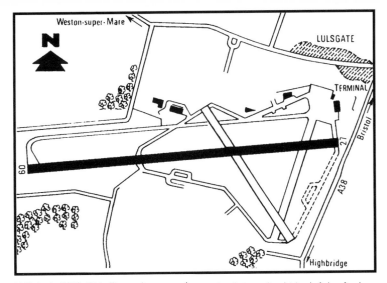

1980s/early 1990s IT traffic was in a general decline at the airport following the demise of Paramount, although this setback has been overcome in recent years.

For many years a point on the Post Office's week-night mail flight network, Bristol continues to play host to aircraft employed on this important task. These vary as contracts are changed, but the Heralds of Channel Express have been regular visitors through the years.

A number of company-operated machines are based at the airport which together with those of the local club and private owners, contribute to the increasing number of movements.

Location and access: Situated 7 miles southwest of Bristol on the A38. Car park charges graduated and are payable at a self-service pay station located opposite the terminal. Bus services link Bristol's Marlborough Street coach station with the airport, taking 40min for the journey before continuing to Weston-super-Mare

Terminal: All of the first floor is devoted to the buffet and bar which has windows overlooking the apron. A new south terminal is to be built as further expansion becomes necessary

Spectator facilities: It seems a long time since the airport boasted a rooftop viewing gallery, a facility long-since absorbed by the expanded buffet area. The latter now provides the only vantage points for viewing in the building, but of course is behind glass. Good landing and

taxying shots can be obtained of aircraft using Runway 27 only a short walk from the terminal and car park

Operators: Scheduled services by Aer Lingus (BAe 146, Fokker 50), Brit Air (ATR42), Brymon Airways (Dash Eight), Delta Air Transport/Sabena (Brasilia), Isles of Scilly Skybus (Twin Otter), Jersey European (Friendship, Short SD3-60), KLM CityHopper (Fokker 50, SAAB SF340). *Charter and IT operators:* Air Europa (Boeing 737), Air Liberte (MD83), Air Malta (Boeing 737), Airtours International (Airbus A320), Airworld (Airbus A320), Air 2000 (Airbus A320, Boeing 757), All Leisure (Airbus A320), Britannia Airways (Boeing 757/767), British Midland (Boeing 737), Futura (Boeing 737), Leisure International (Airbus A320), Monarch Airlines (Boeing 757), Oasis (MD83), Palmair Flightline (BAe 146), Sunway (MD83). *Freight flights:* BAC Express (Short SD3-60), Business Air (SAAB SF340), Channel Express (Herald), Gill Airways (ATR42), Jersey European Airways (Short SD3-60)

Movements (1994): Total 51,598 (air transport 26,141/club 13,570/private 9,235). Total passengers 1,297,448

Runway: 09/27 (6,598ft/2,011m)

Radio frequencies: 133.85MHz (Tower)/120.6MHz (Approach)/124.35MHz (Radar)

Telephone: Bristol (0117) 947 4444

Owned and operated by: Bristol Airport plc

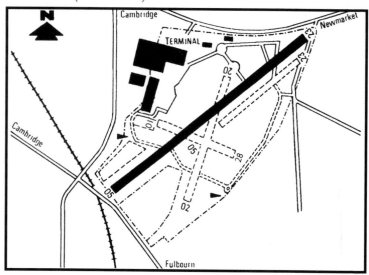

Opened on 8 October 1938, it replaced the smaller field situated a mile or so nearer the city. It not only became the new home for the Cambridge and University Aero Clubs, but also for a training unit for RAF Reserve personnel. During the war, well over 100 Tiger Moths were on the strength of 22 EFTS which operated alongside the Magisters, Masters and Austers in smaller specialised units. All aircraft were maintained by Marshalls, the airfield's owner.

Apart from looking after the local training aircraft, the company became involved in repair and overhaul work for the Air Ministry, particularly with Whitleys, Albemarles, Typhoons and Oxfords. Much work was also done on Mosquito modification and development including radar installation, deck landing conversions and target towing adaptations. The only operational sorties flown from Cambridge were those of Nos 2 and 16 Squadrons' Lysanders during the invasion scares of 1940.

After the war Cambridge reverted to civilian flying training using Tiger Moths, while the Marshall Rapides soon became familiar sights on charter work. RAF Reserve flying continued with 22 RFS, Chipmunks replacing the Tiger Moths in 1950. Military contracts also flourished. Venom assembly and testing in the 1950s was followed by Canberra overhauls and

modifications in the 1960s and 1970s. In 1966 Marshalls became the European centre for civil and military Hercules aircraft, which included the RAF fleet. Painting the latter was a specialised task and was carried out in a new hangar in which temperatures could be controlled. Originally intended to be long-lasting, the two-tone brown and black camouflage was replaced after a few years by green and grey. Yet another change of policy saw a third scheme devised which was of course good news for the paint manufacturers and Marshalls. The fuselage stretch modification to convert the type into a C Mk 3 was undertaken at Cambridge, the last of 29 aircraft being rolled out in November 1985. In 1982 Marshall was given the task of urgently converting some Hercules into tankers for the flight refuelling of similar aircraft. This work was completed in a remarkably short time allowing the type to play a significant role in the South Atlantic airbridge operations leading to the successful outcome of the Falklands campaign.

Lessons learned during the campaign convinced the Ministry of Defence that a large transport was needed for the dual purpose of troop carrier and flight refueller. After evaluating the KC-10A, a suitable type already in service with the USAF, costs were deemed too great. Six second-hand TriStar 500s were therefore bought from British Airways plus another three from Pan American. Marshall was awarded the contract to modify the machines for their new role. It was a long and by no means straightforward task, the first conversion taking almost two years to complete. Meanwhile the unconverted specimens served on the supply runs to the Falklands, awaiting their turn to be modified by the Cambridge company.

In 1990 Marshall won a £30 million contract to continue its maintenance support on the nine-strong RAF TriStar fleet over the next four years. Both major and minor inspections were included plus a non-programmed service in the event of unexpected technical faults. On the strength of the expertise gained during the 1980s, civilian specimens also appeared for overhaul, modification or repaint. British Airways was an early customer in 1986 when its TriStars began to receive interior refits and reskinning where necessary.

Another conversion contract was awarded to the Cambridge company when American International became a customer for eight ex-BA TriStar 200s to be converted into freighters. The work included a strengthened floor and the provision of a large loading door in the forward fuselage. The first machine was delivered in August 1995, with the remainder set to follow at regular intervals. Marshall also has four other orders and is confident of the outcome of negotiations with potential customers.

Since September 1987 a steady stream of BAe 146s have visited Cambridge for various work to be completed. This has included changing cabin configurations, installing galleys and other equipment specified by the operator, or carrying out the latest modifications.

A new type made its appearance at Cambridge in mid-July 1990 when the first of five MD-11s arrived for cabin and flightdeck fitting-out prior to delivery to American Airlines. At one stage in the late 1980s there were plans to build a new jumbo hangar to the north of the field. This was in anticipation of a contract to overhaul Boeing 747s, but when this did not materialise construction of the building was not started. With space already at a premium, it seems likely that some expedient will become necessary if the company is to cope with the growing wide-bodied business.

Marshall has also been a main service centre for Gulfstream aircraft for many years, examples of which are frequently to be seen wearing registrations and colours rare to the UK. Cessna Citations are also handled by the company.

Cambridge has never generated much airline traffic other than on holiday routes. In 1959 Pegasus Airlines offered an Ostend service for a time using Vikings, while Derby Airways introduced their seasonal Jersey operation. From 1964 onwards it became a part of the British Midland network, until in 1972 Air Anglia took over to operate in pool with Intra Airways. A brief attempt with a feeder service to Norwich was unsuccessful and in 1973 Intra assumed sole responsibility for the Jersey schedules. Dakotas were used for some years, but in 1976 Viscounts took over some of the timings, eventually replacing the older machines completely. The Heralds of Express Air Services supplemented the Viscounts in 1979.

The Channel Islands licence changed hands once again in 1981, this time passing to Guernsey Airlines. This carrier was equipped with Short SD3-30s, but when later acquired by British Air Ferries the company added a Viscount to its fleet. In reality, aircraft from either company were then to be found operating the seasonal schedules, an arrangement which ended with the sale of Guernsey Airlines to Aurigny Air Services in October 1987. Dan-Air was contracted for the flights in 1988, with the charter work awarded to Air UK Leisure.

During the next two years the Channel Islands links were handled by both Air UK and Brymon using BAe 146s and Dash Sevens respectively. Both were operated on a non-scheduled basis on Saturdays and Sundays. From 1991 the flights were reduced to a Saturday-only operation during the summer with Air UK employing BAe 146s for the weekly scheduled visits until 1996, when CityFlyer took over.

Cambridge became the terminal for a regular weekday service at last when Suckling Airways took up residence in 1988 with its Dornier 228 after its enforced move from Ipswich. It was a far more suitable operating base for the aircraft, although it did mean that the airline was no longer quite so conveniently placed for its previous customers. Nevertheless, the carrier overcame the problem and successfully continued its regular sorties to Amsterdam and Manchester.

Resident at the airport are the Bulldogs of the Cambridge University Air Squadron which incorporates 5AEF, Cessnas of the Cambridge Aero Club, plus other club, company and privately-owned machines.

Location and access: Situated 2 miles east of the city and south of the A1303 Newmarket Road. Car parking space. Access normally restricted to passengers and friends. A local Cambus route from the railway station or city centre serves the airport at frequent intervals taking about 15min for the journey. Other routes operate from Drummer Street bus station taking about 10min to reach the airport on their way to Newmarket

Terminal: Small but adequate for the number of movements involved. Coffee bar

Spectator facilities: None provided. Around the perimeter there are good vantage points to be found which can be varied according to the position of the sun. Both landing and ground shots are possible, often with uncluttered backgrounds

Operators: Scheduled services by Suckling Airways (Dornier Do228), CityFlyer Express (ATR42/72). *Charter and IT operators:* A number of airlines operate charters in conjunction with special events such as university conferences or classic horse races at nearby Newmarket. These carriers include such as Transavia (Boeing 737), Braathens (Boeing 737), TAT (Fellowship), KLM (Boeing 737),   Air France (Boeing 737), Lufthansa (Boeing 737), Condor (Boeing 737), Crossair (MD87), Meridiana (MD83), TEA Switzerland   (Boeing 737)

Movements (1994): Total 48,290 (air transport 3,357/club 14,857/private 4,059/military 23,299). Total passengers 32,139

Runways: 05/23 (6,4446ft/1,965m), 02/20 (2,943ft/897m – grass), 10/28 (2,280ft/695m – grass) 05/23 (2,80ft/695m – grass)

Radio frequencies: 122.2MHz (Tower)/123.6MHz (Approach)/130.75MHz (Radar)

Telephone: Cambridge (01223) 61133

Owned and operated by: Marshall of Cambridge (Aerospace) Ltd

CARDIFF-INTERNATIONAL (RHOOSE)

The decision to develop Rhoose was taken in 1952 when it became impractical to extend Cardiff's conveniently situated Pengam Moors airfield. The new airport became fully operational on 1 April 1954, after considerable alterations had been made to the buildings, many of which were of wartime origin. Like many others, Rhoose was constructed on the RAF, becoming a base for Spitfire training, 53 OTU using it as a satellite for nearby Llandow from April 1942. This unit left after a year, a lengthy period of time passing before No 7 Air Gunnery School arrived in February 1944. This occupancy ended in August after which, with the exception of a period as a bomb storage depot, the airfield was unused again until its transformation into a civil airport.

Rhoose immediately became the home of Cambrian Airways who in company with Dan-Air and Aer Lingus, slowly expanded the scheduled services from the airport. ITs also began to play a significant part in the increasing traffic figures, until in the mid-1960s it was apparent that the old single-storey buildings were becoming inadequate at peak times. An ambitious development programme resulted in the 1972 opening of the present modern terminal block, a lengthened runway plus updated support services.

International movements were now possible on a larger scale and it was intended that the airport would handle the regional traffic for South Wales and southwest England. However, no progress has been made to fulfil the plans to serve the area across the Bristol Channel. A name change to Cardiff-Wales in 1978 helped to clarify its intended function, since its previous title of Glamorgan (Rhoose) had always proved rather confusing for overseas travellers.

The absorption of Cambrian into British Airways brought about a steady reduction in services through the airport, until in March 1980 all routes were relinquished. The engineering division continued to handle work on One-Eleven 400s for a time and Viscounts until March 1982 when the type was finally withdrawn from British Airways service. They remained a familiar sight at Cardiff, however, since their new owner, British Air Ferries, also took over the maintenance facility. This was not only to relieve their existing works at Southend, but also to acquire premises in which to design and produce a microlight aircraft. The first of these by Dragon Aircraft flew in the summer of 1982.

Both Dan-Air and Aer Lingus continued their association with Rhoose, although the latter's Dublin route was reduced to a single daily flight operated by British Airways in 1979. Air Wales set up its headquarters in 1977 to become the new locally based airline. However, the company ceased operations in 1979 after a take-over by Air Anglia (now Air UK).

As in the case at Bristol, when British Airways gave up the Cardiff routes, Dan-Air was awarded the licences. The airline already served the airport, subsequently becoming the sole operator of schedules. As a stop on the carrier's

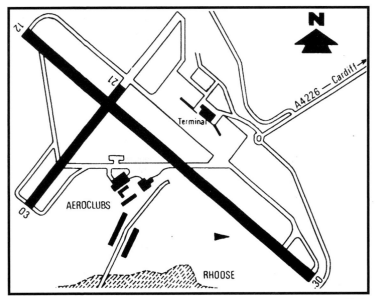

Link City network, Cardiff gained the attentions of Metropolitan Airways when it took over the operation in 1982, but with the company's demise in 1985 the cross-country route ceased to exist. Several attempts have been made to launch a service to Chester in the wake of the defunct Air Wales, but none prospered.

Dan-Air's presence had been steadily reduced until its only contribution in 1990 was a Belfast schedule, but even this was finally withdrawn in 1991. The company's Amsterdam operation was taken over by NetherLines in 1986 while Brown Air reintroduced the Leeds/Glasgow sectors the following spring. The latter airline subsequently became Capital and as such introduced Jersey and Edinburgh links – the latter via Leeds northbound – but with the 360 making a transit stop at Bristol during its southbound travels. It was therefore something of a set-back for the airport when Capital was forced to cease operations at the end of June 1990, thereby further reducing the range of the scheduled services available. It left Ryanair with the twice-weekday flights to Dublin and the two weekend sorties to Guernsey in the hands of Air UK. In the early 1990s Manx decided to create a hub at Cardiff from which to operate a number of domestic and international routes. The airline is now the main scheduled operator with its aircraft flying in British Airways Express

livery, a factor which has been responsible for increased traffic.

Cardiff became the headquarters of Airways International Cymru when it started operations in early 1984 with a pair of One-Elevens. This carrier's declared policy was to concentrate on charters and to lease its small fleet out during the quieter winter months. The airline's career ended in January 1988 but it was replaced at the start of the summer season by newly-formed Amberair. An even shorter lifespan was experienced by this company before it was acquired by Bristol-based Paramount. In the meantime another 737-equipped charter company named Inter European Airways had been formed at Cardiff as a subsidiary of Aspro Travel. Thereafter the machines were to be found at all the familiar holiday airports, but in view of the declining IT market in 1990, the airline decided to diversify its activities. To achieve this aim a number of licence applications were submitted to the CAA covering a vast range of scheduled routes, many of them originating from Cardiff. If approved, it was hoped to launch the new venture during 1991, but a change of policy ended the scheme. In any case, in 1993 Inter European was absorbed by Airtours when the latter's tour operator parent took over Aspro Travel. Nowadays the IT traffic is carried by a variety of UK and foreign airlines, although none have their headquarters at Cardiff International, the present name of the airport.

Long-haul charters have become a regular feature in recent years with transatlantic flights offered from the Welsh airport to the US and Canada throughout the season.

Meanwhile, a steady programme of modernisation and expansion has been undertaken by the airport authorities including an enlarged passenger lounge area and office space for cargo agents in the terminal complex.

In the summer of 1990 it was announced that Cardiff had been chosen by British Airways as the future overhaul centre for its 747-400 fleet. One of the world's largest hangars capable of accepting four of the jets wingtip to wingtip was built on the 29-hectare site. Work commenced in early 1991 so that the first aircraft could arrive for overhaul in 1993.

Local flying clubs operate a selection of light aircraft, while both private and company-owned machines are regular visitors. Rugby internationals, particularly those against France, generate a considerable volume of traffic from both UK and foreign airlines.

The Wales Aircraft Museum first opened at Rhoose in 1976, albeit on a small scale. It was gradually expanded until there were some two dozen aircraft displayed at a site on the approach road to the airport. Unfortunately, the Museum was closed towards the end of 1995 leaving some of the exhibits with uncertain futures. In fact, with very little notice almost all were destroyed as the site was cleared for scrap.

Location and access: Situated 12 miles southwest of Cardiff. Well signposted from the city and M4 Junction 33 via A4232 and A4050. Car park charges graduated. Airport Express bus service X91 operates hourly in both directions between the terminal and Cardiff Central bus and rail station, Monday to Saturday. Service 145 takes over on Sunday. It takes 30min to complete the journey

Terminal: Contains lounge, restaurant, bar, buffet and shop

Spectator facilities: Access to a good viewing terrace overlooking the apron can be gained either from the second floor of the terminal or via external stairs. Admission is free. All movements can be readily seen, while photographic opportunities vary with the stand used. Generally there are few problems but mornings are preferable in sunny conditions. A 135mm lens is useful but not essential

Operators: Scheduled services by KLM CityHopper (Fokker 50, SAAB SF340), Manx Airlines (BAe ATP, 146, Jetstream 41), Ryanair (Boeing 737). *Charter and IT operators:* Air Malta (Boeing 737), Airtours International (Airbus A320), Air Transat (Boeing 757), Air VIA (Tu-154), Air World (Airbus A320), All Leisure (Airbus A320), Aurigny (Short SD3-60), AviaReps/Air Atlanta Iceland (Boeing 737), Britannia Airways (Boeing 757/767), Futura (Boeing 737), Monarch Airlines (Boeing 757), Oasis (MD83), Pegasus (Boeing 737), Sunway (MD83), Transwede (MD87). *Cargo flights:* BAC Express (Short SD3-60), Channel Express (Herald)

Movements (1994): Total 55,742 (air transport 16,203/club 27,644/private 6,048). Total passengers 1,032,276

Runways: 03/21 (3,670ft/1,119m) 12/30 (7,700ft/2,347m)

Radio frequencies: 125.0MHz (Tower)/125.85MHz (Approach)

Telephone: Rhoose (01446) 711111

Operated by: Cardiff International Airport Ltd

CARLISLE (CROSBY)

Of wartime construction, the airfield was first used by the Hurricanes of 59 OTU in February 1941. Training of a different kind was commenced in August of the following year by 9 OTU of Coastal Command equipped with Whitleys and Beaufighters. The airfield became a part of Transport Command in August 1944, this time becoming the base of 109 OCU with its Dakotas. The unit later was renumbered 1383 TSCU still retaining the same type, remaining so until disbanded in May 1946. The airfield became unoccupied soon after and although the town of Carlisle was served almost every summer after scheduled services were reintroduced postwar, the airfield originally employed was Silloth.

In the 1960s operations were moved to Crosby which was renovated and renamed Carlisle Airport. Control responsibility was in the hands of Casair Ltd, a company engaged in charter work and flying training. In 1967 Dan-Air restarted the traditional seasonal route to the Isle of Man, at first using Dakotas but in 1970 introducing Ambassadors. The service originated at Newcastle, calling at Crosby *en route*. Two years later saw the operation subcontracted to Kestrel for the season, while Dan-Air introduced a second route from the

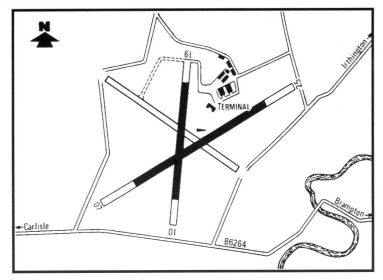

airport, this time to Jersey with BAe (HS) 748s.

In the meantime the Oxford-based CSE company had taken over Casair and the airfield operation in July 1969. This resulted in a build-up of flying training activities, but a cessation of charter work. The seasonal schedules continued, although Crosby became a terminal instead of merely a transit stop. In 1979, Intra took over the licence from Dan-Air in exchange for their Jersey-Staverton route. That summer the company employed a Viscount on the Jersey service, but due to the uncertainty of Carlisle's future, the airline moved the northern terminal to Prestwick for the 1980 season. By this time Jersey European had become the operator, again using a Viscount for the long haul south. Yet another reorganisation left JEA as a Bandeirante/Twin Otter operator, with the result that no Carlisle or Prestwick service was flown in 1981/82. Scheduled services did return to Carlisle, however, when in March 1982 the airport became part of a short-lived bus stop type of operation flown by Air Ecosse to connect Liverpool, Blackpool, Barrow, Carlisle, Glasgow and Aberdeen with a twice weekly Twin Otter flight. During the summer of 1982, the airline served the Isle of Man, again with Twin Otters. None of this was particularly profitable, so not surprisingly the services were discontinued. Carlisle was not forsaken by the airline, however, because it included the airport as a transit stop on a new route from Dundee to Heathrow in 1984. Using Short SD3-60s,

load factors were not encouraging, so the operation was taken over by Euroair in November 1985. While its 748s reversed the trend by providing a more comfortable trip for the passengers, nevertheless the service was withdrawn in early 1987 following a reorganisation within Euroair and the decision to discontinue its involvement with schedules. As a result the only regular flight from Carlisle became the seasonal once-weekly Viscount service to Jersey provided by British Air Ferries.

Fresh hopes were raised during the summer of 1987 for the revival of the London link which, when suspended, was just beginning to be fully appreciated by businessmen in particular. An application by Brymon to take over the licence was made to the CAA in the middle of the year, but instead the airline decided to concentrate its resources on the London City project with no further involvement in Carlisle. During 1988 Air Furness began regular links with the Isle of Man using an Islander and also proposed to introduce other routes. However, during the year the airline was forced to cease operations due to circumstances beyond its control, spelling an end to commercial flying at the Cumbrian airport for the time being. In early 1990 British Northern Airways announced its intention to operate schedules from Carlisle to Belfast, Dublin, Brussels and Heathrow. A request for a charter series to Jersey was later withdrawn. If successful in its applications, BNA expected to employ ATR42s for the services, but no action could be taken before the CAA was satisfied with the financial state of the company. Presumably this was never achieved because no more was heard of the airline's plans.

In 1993 there was a revival of the London scheduled link when New Air (not to be confused with the Danish carrier of the same name) began thrice-weekdaily services with a Jetstream 31. Unusually, the company selected Biggin Hill as the London terminal for this latest attempt to link the border city with the south, but as with its predecessors, the operation did not survive for very long. Subsequently the Gill Airways mail flights each weekday have remained the only commercial flight in the last year or two, although the airport management still hopes that a carrier will accept the challenge to provide a much-needed connection with either of the main London airports or Manchester. A number of private, military and company aircraft regularly use the facilities, but for the moment would-be airline travellers have to take the cross-country A69 road to Newcastle or south on the M6 to Manchester.

Location and access: Situated 5 miles east-northeast of Carlisle off A689 to Brampton. A local Ribble bus from the city bus station takes some 20min for the journey, but it then involves a walk of about one mile from the nearest alighting point

Terminal: Small building alongside the tower contains bar and buffet

Spectator facilities: Good viewing in the vicinity of the terminal which also provides a photographic vantage point. Landing shots are possible at the threshold of the runway in use

Operators: Scheduled services suspended. Mail flights by Gill Airways (Short SD3-30/SD3-60). A number of light aircraft are based at the airport

Movements (1994): Total 30,378 (air transport 425/test & training 12,450/club 11,744/private 3,878). Total passengers 1,109

Runways: 07/25 (6,026ft/1,837m), 01/19 (4,225ft/1,288m)

Radio frequency: 123.6MHz (Tower and Approach)

Telephone: Carlisle (01228) 573641

Operated by: Carlisle City Council

COVENTRY (BAGINTON)

Unlike many of the municipalities that were struggling to provide a local airport in the 1930s, Coventry's authorities were able to benefit from the presence of an ambitious company already in residence on the outskirts of the city. Although Armstrong Whitworth possessed a small field from which it flew its

lighter products, since the manufacturer was turning its attention towards a bomber for the RAF, the idea of a larger facility nearby met with its approval. Work was already well advanced with a design to meet the requirements of the Air Ministry's specification B3/34, the first prototype flying in March 1936. By the time

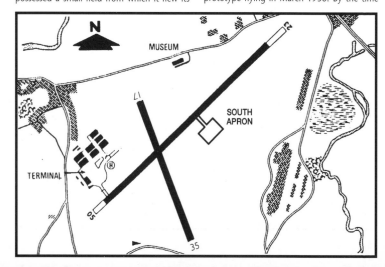

that the second took to the air 11 months later, the Baginton factory had begun work. Taking the name of Whitley, progress with its production was slow and consequently the type was being overtaken by modern developments. At the start of the war, proposals were made that Armstrong Whitworth should produce the new twin-engined Manchester, but this and a similar scheme involving Halifaxes was abandoned in favour of later variants of the ageing Whitley. During the period from March 1937 to June 1943 the company delivered 1,812 examples of the type, most of them flying from Baginton.

From this point attention was turned to producing the radial-engined Lancaster II, although the airfield was also used for testing other versions of the bomber. Once the war in Europe was over, a contract was awarded to the manufacturer to bring the more plentiful Merlin-powered variant up to Far East standard. Lincolns were also included in this programme, a type built by Armstrong Whitworth between 1945 and 1948. Civil aviation was not forgotten, the company building an advanced flying wing intended for use as a mail carrier and the Apollo turboprop airliner. Prototypes of the latter were flown from Baginton but no production was forthcoming, the rival Viscount securing all orders.

Meanwhile links with Hawker Siddeley brought Meteor production to Coventry, while the design staff worked on various bomber and fighter products. Although nothing came of most of these, the company's nightfighter development of the Meteor 7 was adopted by the RAF. Starting with the Mk 11, all of the aircraft destined for this role were built at Baginton as were indeed the Sapphire-powered Hunter 2s and 5s. Surprisingly, until October 1960 there was no hard runway at the airfield, most of the jet types flying from Bitteswell. It befell the Argosy to become the last machine to be constructed at Baginton, but this transport was only produced in small numbers before the factory closed on 16 July 1965.

Air transport movements had never been particularly numerous at Coventry although small carriers from time to time had introduced schedules to the Channel Islands and the Isle of Man. Provision of the runway was an improvement which was essential if the airport was to attract other airlines. It helped to encourage British United Air Ferries to start a car ferry service to Calais in 1964, an enterprise which lasted three years or so. A second attempt using the larger Carvair on a Channel Islands sector was launched in 1972, but this

too only survived until the end of the following year. From this point until the early 1980s the sole operator of a scheduled passenger service was British Midland with a seasonal operation to Jersey. There was an increase in the spring of 1982 when the resident company, Air Commuter, was awarded a licence for a Coventry-Paris link, the inaugural flight being made in May using a Bandeirante leased from Genair. The latter introduced its own schedules from Baginton on 5 April 1983, when the Short SD3-30s maintaining the Liverpool-Gatwick service began to call en route. In the meantime the Paris-bound passengers with Air Commuter were now travelling in a Jetstream contracted from Peregrine prior to delivery of the airline's own machine. Poor loads sadly brought a swift end to the Genair service on 13 August, although the company remained optimistic that it would return to Coventry in the future.

During May 1984 Air Commuter changed its name to Venture Airways, at the same time replacing its equipment with an HS 748 configured with a first class layout. Also appearing that summer were the newly acquired Viscount 700s of Janus Airways, the company which operated the air portion of Hards Travel's coach-air holidays to the Continent. Unfortunately this level of commercial activity was not to continue for very long. On 31 July it was announced that Venture Airways had suspended its Paris schedule, the last sortie by the 748 G-VAJK taking place on the previous day. In due course a liquidator was appointed, thereby formally removing any chance of a resumption. Janus reverted to being an all-Herald operator during the following year, but a contraction of its type of business forced Hards to sell the carrier to Euroair in the spring of 1986. Charter flights by the latter frequented Coventry during the year, particularly on sectors to Eire. Applications were submitted to the CAA for scheduled licences to these destinations, but a change in company policy left the future of such operations in doubt. None the less, a scheduled service to Dublin was launched in 1989 but it was flown by a Ryanair One-Eleven. The limited programme proved sufficiently popular for the frequency to be increased to a daily service (except Saturday) in 1990, achieved by staging the Stansted flight via the Midlands airport. A Sunday service to Knock was also launched using an ATR42, but the Irish services were discontinued and Ryanair concentrated its activities at nearby Birmingham.

For many years the seasonal summer trips to the Channel Islands almost became a tradition.

Both British Midland and British Air Ferries operated the flights, the latter employing Viscounts for its charter services. Eventually BMA was alone on the route for several seasons, until in 1990 it also removed the sector from its network.

In due course locally-based Air Corbiere introduced scheduled services to Guernsey and Jersey using Titans and a solitary Metro from 1992, but even these were withdrawn after a couple of years. Orientair then launched an ambitious scheduled programme to link Coventry with Dublin, Gloucestershire and the Channel Islands, but these soon suffered a similar fate. There are now no regular passenger services from the airport, but fortunately these losses have been compensated to some extent by an increase in cargo flights.

Coventry became the main base of Air Atlantique early in 1986, its DC-3 fleet and Bristol Freighter moving in from Stansted. Thereafter freight charters kept the machines busy, while passenger pleasure flights continued to be popular. In the early part of 1987 the airport became the base for a pair of DC-6s acquired by the company for longer range cargo work.

General aviation is also well catered for with several operators and maintenance companies in residence. A change of airport operator was planned during 1982, but after much deliberation the City Council continued in the role. At last there were signs that it wished to develop the airport rather than close it. Modest extensions to the terminal were completed by the summer of 1985, going a long way to easing the congestion particularly at times of diversions or charters using larger aircraft.

Also located at Coventry is the Midland Air Museum, which contains amongst its growing number of interesting exhibits the locally-built Argosy G-APRL. Operated by Air Bridge for Elan International, the aircraft was delivered to its birthplace on 20 February 1987 to begin its retirement alongside the new 10,000sq ft 'Sir Frank Whittle Jet Heritage Centre'.

Location and access: Situated 3 miles south of Coventry off A45. Car park charged on a pay-and-display basis. Midland Red provides a bus route which links Coventry (Pool Meadow bus station) with Leamington via the airport access road taking some 15min for the journey from the city

Terminal: Single-storey building containing lounge area. Vending machines are available for drinks

Spectator facilities: None provided. Photography and viewing possible from the short-term car park area and vantage points on airfield perimeter

Operators: Scheduled services suspended. *Cargo operators:* Atlantic Air Cargo (DC-3, DC-6, Electra), British World Airlines (Viscount), Channel Express (Electra, Friendship, Herald), El Air Exports (Friendship), Emerald Air (HS 748), Farner Air Transport (Friendship), Hunting Cargo (Electra), Ratioflug (Friendship). Passenger charters are handled from time to time, particularly when there are special events in progress locally

Movements (1994): Total 56,683 (air transport 6,949/positioning 3,073/test & training 30,618/club 9,524/private 6,410). Total passengers 3,371

Runways: 05/23 (5,300ft/1,615m), 17/35 (2,673ft/815m)

Radio frequencies: 124.8MHz (Tower)/119.25MHz (Approach)/122.0MHz (Radar)

Telephone: Coventry (01203) 301717

Operated by: Coventry City Council

DUNDEE (RIVERSIDE)

As the name suggests, this small airport occupies a narrow strip of land between the Tay and the main road. It was opened in 1963 on the site of former playing fields. Scheduled services from Dundee started after a couple of years or so when Strathair received approval for a Dundee-Edinburgh route, later expanded to take in Inverness and Prestwick. The sector serving the latter was started in July 1966 and was intended to act as a feeder for international flights. It did not receive much support, however, which meant that after two months the service was withdrawn.

Also in July another route was introduced, this time to Glasgow with British Eagle employing a Dove. Again the idea was to connect with the carrier's London trunk services. The airline carried on for almost two years, but when Autair began a Dundee-London operation, inevitably support quickly disappeared and with it the link with Glasgow.

Although Autair had attempted to use Riverside, the field suffered from waterlogging making the use of 748s or Heralds impractical. As a result and two years of negotiations later, the airline received permission to use RAF

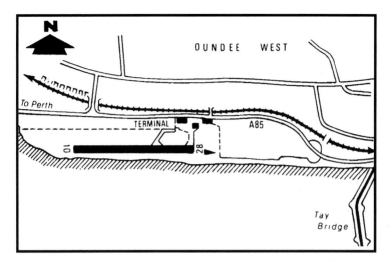

Leuchars as the Dundee terminal, commencing in April 1968. The enterprise was again short-lived since the following year Autair abandoned all scheduled work when it became involved entirely with ITs as Court Line.

After an inactive period, the airport came to life again in 1971 when the Glasgow route was reopened, this time by Loganair using an Islander. Although subsidised by Dundee Corporation, the airline could not absorb the increasing losses resulting in the link once again being severed, this time in May 1975.

Throughout its life as an airport, Riverside had been an all-grass field. Following a decision taken in 1977, a tarmac runway was provided which has allowed more reliable operations. Schedules subsequently returned to Dundee with Air Ecosse offering Manchester and Aberdeen services, followed in 1984 by a London link after many years. Using Short SD3-60s, two return trips were made each weekday via Carlisle, the timings such that a day trip to the capital was practical. However, the airline found difficulty in bringing the route into profitability, so in November 1985 Euroair took over the service. Immediately there was an improvement in the loads carried, probably due to the greater comfort offered by the HS 748 employed. However, a change of policy in early 1987 resulted in the carrier withdrawing from the scheduled scene, although it continued to operate the services to Manchester and Aberdeen on behalf of Air Ecosse throughout the latter's period of reorganisation.

During the year Euroair's Scottish operations were taken over by Business Air, a new airline formed at Aberdeen for the purpose. A service between Dundee and Esbjerg was inaugurated in the spring of 1988 while the regular sorties to Aberdeen and Manchester continued with Bandeirantes. Traffic was encouraging and by 1990 the company was actively considering the acquisition of a larger type. This was achieved during the year when the Swiss regional carrier Crossair transferred a SAAB SF340 after taking a financial interest in the Scottish airline. Applications were also made to the CAA for several new routes including Birmingham, Liverpool, Edinburgh and East Midlands, but none were ever started. The only direct flight available to Dundee travellers is a twice-daily link with Edinburgh, but by using the onward service to Manchester, a range of convenient connections are available to widen the scope considerably. There has been no further interest shown in the dormant Heathrow sector, although in 1987 Brymon had been expected to start the service with a leased HS 748. However, after a change of policy the airline dropped the scheme.

Location and access: Situated 2 miles west of the city centre between the north bank of the Firth of Tay and the A85
Terminal: Small single-storey building containing waiting area. Drinks machine provided

Spectator facilities: None provided. Views of the apron can be obtained from the east side of the terminal, but due to the growth of the shrubbery this vantage point is becoming less useful. Photography is possible through the perimeter fence to the west and all movements can be readily observed
Operator: Business Air (SAAB SF340)

Movements (1994): Total 37,104 (air transport 2,106/club 30,249/private 2,021/military 1,388). Total passengers 22,225
Runway: 10/28 (3,608ft/1,100m)
Radio frequency: 122.9MHz (Tower and Approach)
Telephone: Dundee (01382) 643242
Operated by: Tayside Regional Council

EAST MIDLANDS (CASTLE DONINGTON)

Castle Donington was destined to became the satellite airfield for Wymeswold, opening as such on 1 January 1943. Accordingly part of 28 OTU was transferred to the new station, using its Wellingtons for the urgent task of aircrew training. A few Lysanders and Martinets were also on strength for target towing purposes, later replaced by Hurricanes. The first crews passed out in June 1943, making sorties over enemy territory at the end of the training courses prior to joining front line squadrons.

In October 1944, the unit was disbanded, but Castle Donington then became host to 108 OTU, sharing its Dakotas with the parent airfield at Wymeswold. The output target was 24 crews every three weeks from courses of 12 weeks duration, resulting in a considerable build-up of flying hours at the bases.

With the war in Europe over, the unit was renumbered 1382 Transport Conversion Unit on 10 August 1945, but retaining the same aircraft. By this time, Transport Command was busy ferrying supplies and personnel to and from the Far and Middle East areas, a task in which Castle Donington's Dakotas also became involved. However, by September 1946, the much reduced air crew requirement meant that the airfield was no longer needed and therefore it was closed down.

In the 1950s it was realised that the existing airport at Burnaston had limited development potential. Serious thought was given to finding a successor, the eventual choice being the long-abandoned Castle Donington. Although employing the old site, very little proved of use during the conversion. Even the original main runway had to be completely relaid, as did the various taxiways and most of the internal roads. When it was opened in April 1965, East Midlands became the first new municipal airport to have been constructed in Britain since the war. Soon afterwards British Midland opened its operating base to become the first resident airline. The airport was also chosen as the base of the Argosy and Merchantman-equipped airline Air Bridge Carriers, while in

1980 the newly formed IT carrier Orion Airways began its commercial career. Scheduled services were also introduced by Alidair, a company which began charter operations from East Midlands in 1972, later trading as Inter City Airlines until its demise in August 1983.

While British Midland still provides schedules from the airport, other companies have joined it from time to time through the years. NetherLines introduced an Amsterdam sector, while Air Ecosse was successful in acquiring the Scottish licences previously held by Inter City. However, it was not long before difficulties led to these domestic routes being flown by Peregrine Air Services on behalf of the holder. Eventually the latter carrier, under its new name of Aberdeen Airways, was awarded the licences in its own right. After several years' absence a Dublin route was reinstated in the mid-1980s, this time using the Short SD3-60s of Aer Lingus. In due course this type was replaced by the SAAB SF340, but during 1995 another change found the Fokker 50 on the sector. At the end of the same year the latest scheduled carrier began operations at East Midlands. The newcomer was Community Express, which offered three daily return flights to Gatwick via Birmingham, together with a similar number of sorties to Belfast City, both services flown by Short SD3-60s. The Irish schedule filled the void left when the previous operator, Genesis Airways, ceased trading earlier in the year.

Although starting life exclusively as a charter airline, in 1986 Orion successfully gained permission to fly schedules from East Midlands to Palma and Malaga, both destinations already frequently visited during the course of its IT work. The airline had quickly won a reputation for its quality of service, so when the news was released that Orion was to be integrated into Britannia during 1989, it came as a surprise to the industry and public alike. It was not long before the familiar livery and titles disappeared from aircraft and buildings at East Midlands because the new owner understandably intended to concentrate its activities at its Luton base. Naturally the scheduled licences were transferred to Britannia without interruption, but at the end of the 1990 summer season the airline decided to withdraw from this market in favour of its charter work.

In the meantime the previous management of Orion had formed TEA UK with its base at Birmingham, but although successful, due to the failure of its parent company in Belgium, the airline was forced to cease trading. In 1992 the same team formed Excalibur Airways which introduced the Airbus A320 to IT work, a role for which it subsequently proved to be well suited. Nevertheless, despite the carrier's headquarters being at East Midlands, it was not until 1995 that one of the fleet was based at the airport. Later that year it was announced that the Scottish tour operator Globespan had bought the company since it needed extra capacity for its long-haul ITs. Excalibur had already announced that it would be operating two DC-10-30s in 1996, with the original four A320s exchanged for others of the breed or their equivalent, the state of the leisure market influencing the decision.

Field Aircraft has also been a resident of East Midlands for many years. Nowadays the company is responsible for the installation of flightdeck instrumentation, avionics, wiring, passengers cabin interiors and final painting as required by the contracted customer. Most of the Jetstream 31s built passed through the plant, having been ferried from Prestwick in a basic state. After some 20 days, the aircraft were flown back to the manufacturer in readiness for delivery. Refurbishment and painting of BAe 146s returning after lease is another activity which has been carried out by the company through the years.

From the time that its operational life began, the airport has developed into an important centre, serving not only neighbouring Derby and Nottingham, but many other towns thanks to its very convenient position just off the M1.

Recognising the potential, the authorities commenced a major expansion programme in 1981 to give additional cargo facilities, together with a large apron extension. Once completed, attention was turned to the passenger terminal with the result that a much improved building became available to handle the growing traffic. A western taxiway was also laid to eliminate the need for back-tracking along the runway.

Other changes were constantly introduced, but it was in 1995 that Phase One of a new £8 million terminal extension began. The work included an expanded check-in hall, a modern baggage handling system, together with an enlarged arrivals facility. Construction was expected to be completed before the start of the 1996 summer programme, but in the meantime a certain amount of reorganisation was necessary, especially to the area in front of the building. Phase Two was due to begin before the end of 1995 and was aimed to completely transform the existing premises with improved catering facilities, additional shops and a more spacious departure lounge.

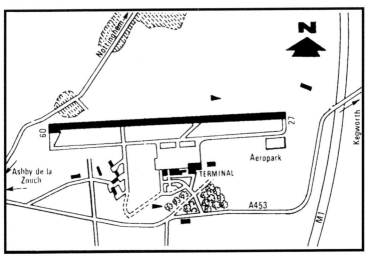

East Midlands has always been regarded as an important cargo airport from where one of the first express parcel links was started in the early 1980s. Nevertheless, it was not until the early 1990s that the movement of freight began to grow rapidly in volume, helped by the arrival of United Parcels and its regular services from the US and Germany. Others very much in evidence are Hunting Cargo, DHL and Lufthansa, all making use of the new 25,000sqm freight apron which was completed in the spring of 1995. This has already shown signs of being insufficient, so plans are now in hand for further growth. A runway extension is also under consideration so that the use of larger, quieter types with greater capacity can be encouraged.

As the airport grew so the valuable space occupied by the spectators' enclosure and the Loughborough and Leicester Aircraft Museum was needed. This could easily have meant the end of the excellent viewing arrangements enjoyed for some years, but instead the authorities agreed to provide an Aeropark to combine both the facility for observing the airport movements with static exhibits and an exhibition hall. Completed in 1984, the enterprise has proved very successful with the exhibits including a Varsity, Vulcan, S-55, the SA-1 Sheriff and an Argosy. However, in the spring of 1996 it appeared likely that the facility is to be closed and the site cleared.

Location and access: Situated 2 miles from M1 Junction 24 via A453. Ample parking space, graduated charges. Various local bus services connect the airport with Derby (12 miles), Nottingham (14 miles) and Leicester (20 miles). From the airport terminal bus stop it is about a 10min walk to the signposted Aeropark
Terminal: A modern two-storey building containing a buffet on the ground floor, plus a choice of eating styles within two areas on the first floor. There are two bars in the public section plus a shop with a good selection of aviation books
Spectator facilities: The Aeropark is located at the eastern end of the runway and is reached from a point near to the airport entrance. There is a fixed fee for a car which includes all occupants. From the grass-covered mounds excellent viewing is possible, while photographs of aircraft on the adjacent taxiway or landing on Runway 27 can be obtained, but sadly, closure of the area is a distinct possibility.
Operators: Scheduled services by Aer Lingus Commuter (Fokker 50), British Midland (BAe ATP, Boeing 737, Fokker 70, Jetstream 41), Business Air (SAAB SF340), Community Express (Jetstream 31 Short SD3-60). *Charter and IT operators:* AviaReps/Air Atlanta (Boeing 737), Air Europa (Boeing 737), Air Malta (Boeing 737), Airtours International (Airbus A320, Boeing 757), Air VIA (Tu-154B), Air World (Airbus A320), American Trans Air (TriStar), Britannia Airways (Boeing 757/767), British Midland (Boeing 737), Futura (Boeing 737), Monarch Airlines (Airbus A300, Boeing 757), Oasis (MD83), Spanair (MD83), Sunway (MD83), Transwede (MD87). *Cargo flights:* Aurigny Air Services (Short SD3-60), BAC Express (Short SD3-60), Channel Express (Electra, Friendship, Herald), DHL (Boeing 727, Convair 580, DC-8), Gill Airways (Short SD3-60), Hunting Cargo (Electra), Island Flug (Metro), Lufthansa (Boeing 737), Titan Airways (Short SD3-60), United Parcel Service (Boeing 767, DC-8)
Movements (1994): Total 61,525 (air transport 32,954/positioning 1,909/test & training 1,713/club 16,929/private 6,244/military 1,091). Total passengers 1,622,636
Runway: 09/27 (7,480ft/2,280m)
Radio frequencies: 124.0MHz (Tower)/119.65MHz (Approach)
Telephone: Derby (01332) 810621
Operated by: East Midlands International Airport plc

Below:
The mound provided in East Midlands' Aeropark enables photographs to be taken over the fence. British Midland operates the ATP on schedules from the airport. *A. S. Wright*

EDINBURGH (TURNHOUSE)

Turnhouse opened in 1915, becoming the most northerly of the defence stations in World War 1. Between the wars it became the home of No 603 (City of Edinburgh) Squadron, for the majority of its peacetime existence equipped in turn with DH-9As, Westland Wapitis, Hawker Harts and Hind light bombers. A change of role found the squadron with Spitfires at the outbreak of war, the airfield at the same time coming under the control of Fighter Command. Hard runways were laid permitting it to be used on a regular basis by squadrons resident for varying periods of time.

Although scheduled passenger services began in 1947, it was some years before traffic built up. By the mid-fifties Viscounts began to replace the Pionairs on the main routes, at the same time offering a modest increase in frequencies. A brand-new terminal was opened in 1956, which received a further extension five years later. The mid-sixties saw Comets employed on a few prestige flights to counter the growing competition, but the remainder of the timings were maintained by Vanguards and Viscounts.

It became apparent by the late sixties that major development was necessary if Turnhouse was to cope with the increasing traffic created by the oil business. The BAA assumed control in April 1971, shortly afterwards launching a programme to provide a new runway and terminal building.

British Airways was therefore able to introduce a shuttle service to London in 1976 using Tridents without restriction. The following year saw the completion of the terminal designed to cope with 1,500,000 passengers each year. International routes available dwindled in the early 1980s until only Amsterdam and Dublin were served non-stop, but gradually new destinations in Germany were added by BA while Air France returned to the airport with a Paris link. There is a reasonable choice of domestic services on offer, the most significant addition coming with the award of a licence to British Midland enabling the carrier to operate to Heathrow in competition with the British Airways shuttle.

For many years British Caledonian operated a regular schedule to Gatwick, but with the take-over by BA, the licence was duly awarded to Air UK. Marketed as the Sterling service, the company introduced the BAe 146 to the route in October 1988 and was rewarded with traffic

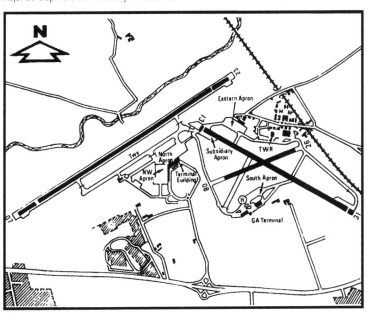

figures considerably better than those experienced by the previous operator. Edinburgh was also served by Chieftain Airways during its short career in 1987; a duty taken over by Scottish European in November 1988 when it began serving Brussels and Frankfurt. Activities continued into 1990 but the company was then forced to end its operations.

Nowadays Edinburgh is well served on the London routes with frequent services to Heathrow, Gatwick and Stansted by British Midland, British Airways and Air UK. In November 1995 a new low-cost airline, easyJet, added to the selection when it introduced a thrice-daily link with Luton using Boeing 737s. The airport also continues to be an important freight centre, particularly with the movement of overnight mail and parcels traffic.

Location and access: Situated 8 miles west of Edinburgh, reached via signposted access on A8 midway between the Maybury and Newbridge roundabouts. Car park charges graduated. Lothian Regional Transport provides a link with the city centre at Waverley about every 30min. Journey time is approximately 25min
Terminal: Contains large buffet, bar, restaurant, shop and lounge area
Spectator facilities: A gallery is provided along the front of the second floor of the terminal, admission free. Overlooking the apron and runway, it provides good opportunities for both viewing and photography although a telephoto lens is desirable for most shots. Facing north, there is no problem with the sun should it be in evidence. Access is signposted via internal stairs and an internal observation area which is useful in times of inclement weather. Other vantage points exist near the runway thresholds and the old terminal building, now used as a cargo centre

Operators: Scheduled services by Aer Lingus (BAe 146, Fokker 50), Air France (Boeing 737), Air UK (BAe 146, Fokker 50, Fokker 100, Friendship), British Airways (BAe ATP, Boeing 737/757/767), British Midland (Boeing 737, Fokker 70), Brymon Airways (Dash Eight), Business Air (SAAB SF340), Crossair (Avro RJ85), easyJet (Boeing 737), Gill Airways (Short SD3-60), Loganair (Short SD3-60), Manx Airlines (Jetstream 41), Sabena/Delta Air Transport (Avro RJ85). *Charter and IT operators:* Air Europa (Boeing 737), Air Malta (Boeing 737), Air Transat (Boeing 757), Air VIA (Tu-154B), American Trans Air (Boeing 757), Austrian Airlines (MD83), Balkan (Tu-154B), Britannia Airways (Boeing 757/767), Eurocypria (Airbus A320), Finnair (MD83), Oasis (MD83), Spanair (MD83). *Cargo flights:* Atlantic Air Transport (Electra), BAC Express (Shorts SD3-60), British World Airlines (Viscount), Business Air (SAAB SF340), Channel Express (Electra), DHL (Convair 580), Emerald Airways (HS748), Flightline (Bandeirante), Gill Airways (ATR42), TNT (BAe 146)
Movements (1994): Total 110,265 (air transport 61,080/club 20,196/private 6,044/military 19,367). Total passengers 3,116,559
Runways: 07/25 (8,400ft/2,560m), 13/31 (6,000ft/1,829m), 08/26 (2,982ft/909m)
Radio frequencies: 118.7MHz (Tower)/121.2MHz (Approach)
Telephone: Edinburgh (0131) 333 1000
Operated by: Edinburgh Airport Ltd

EXETER (CLYST HONITON)

Officially opened on 30 June 1938, although both Jersey Airways and Railway Air Services had included Exeter in their route network from mid-1937. A Bristol-Plymouth-Land's End-Scilly Islands service was routed via Exeter by Great Western & Southern Airlines from May 1939, but at the outbreak of war these civil flights were suspended. The airfield handled various miscellaneous units until it became an official RAF station on 6 July 1940. Thereafter fighter squadrons came and went, Nos 87 and 213 serving during the Battle of Britain.

In April 1944 the airfield assumed the identity of Station 463 for the benefit of the USAAF. The 440th Troop Carrier Group arrived with its C-47s in readiness for the D-Day

activities and subsequent sorties over Normandy. By August the war had moved on, leaving Exeter to receive the Masters and Hotspurs of 3 Glider Training School. This unit remained until August 1945, its place taken for short periods by operational squadrons including the Meteors of No 222 Squadron.

The Ministry of Civil Aviation took over control of the airfield on 1 January 1947, although military aircraft were to be seen for a long time to come. The Tiger Moths and Chipmunks of 10 Reserve Flying School remained until disbanded in 1954, while 3 Civil Anti-Aircraft Co-operation Unit used a variety of aircraft types during its long existence at Exeter.

In 1952 Jersey Airlines reintroduced the

Channel Islands routes, which still remain popular today albeit with different carriers. A London link was attempted briefly by Olley Air Services about the same period, followed later by services to Gatwick, Newquay, Plymouth and the Scillies flown for a time by British Westpoint. In the late 1950s/early 1960s both Starways and North-South Airlines connected Exeter to the north, while South West Aviation came on the scene much later with a Cherbourg service in 1970.

The demise of all these airlines in some cases saw the end of the routes; in others the licences were taken over by the next ambitious carrier. British Island Airways and Brymon Airways provided the services during most of the 1970s to such places as Belfast, Channel Islands, Dublin and the Scillies. The pair were joined in 1978 by Air Westward, which began by operating Titans to Amsterdam, Gatwick, Glasgow, Paris and later Brussels. The company did not survive very long, with the result that BIA took over the ailing airline after 10 months or so, operating it under the name of BIA-Air West. By October 1979 it was common knowledge that BIA and Air Anglia plus associated carriers were to merge to form Air UK. Exeter became the headquarters of the combined six-strong Bandeirante fleet, the type then used on routes requiring less capacity. In March 1981 this group became the Air UK Commuter Services division, operating a pruned network at frequencies likely to attract businessmen in particular. Gradually Exeter saw the routes on offer contract, until by the summer of 1982 only a daily Jersey service and a weekday Gatwick/Rotterdam through flight were available in the Air UK network. Brymon continued to serve the airport throughout the decade with its Twin Otters connecting Exeter with Plymouth and London (Gatwick), until in 1989 most flights were upgraded to the Dash Seven. However, one of the smaller machines was retained because the length of the runway at St Mary's meant that the airline was restricted to using the type for the Isles of Scilly services. The operation finally ended at the conclusion of the 1990 summer season when Brymon disposed of its Twin Otter. Later the carrier applied for the Channel Islands licences vacated by Air UK, but at the same time suspended its Gatwick service due to rising costs.

As Jersey European expanded, it chose the Devon airport for its administration centre in January 1986, although this did not mean any less commitment to the Channel Islands. Two routes were added to the network, namely those to Belfast and Dublin – both one-time Air UK territory, but now intended as a means of feeding Irish traffic to Jersey and Guernsey – destinations regularly served by JEA. In the event the route to the Republic was later dropped, but a twice-daily link with Manchester proved more successful for a time. The airline eventually discontinued the service, but the sector later passed into the hands of Eagle European, a carrier which also included Dublin in its network before ceasing operations in 1994. The choice of scheduled services still remains quite small, but at least Irish services were restored by Air South West by linking both the Irish capital and Cork with Exeter. Flights are timed to give an opportunity for onward journeys to Boston, Edinburgh and Glasgow using Dublin as a transit point. Travellers are also able to fly to St Mary's with Isles of Scilly Skybus which uses either its Islanders or

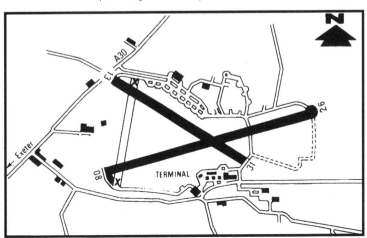

Twin Otter for the scheduled trips.

Westcountry Aircraft Servicing carries out regular maintenance and overhaul work on piston and turboprop airliners belonging to various carriers. The airport also frequently serves as a haven for migrating Short SD3-30s and 3-60s. A number of these types are often to be seen displaying evidence of past operators as they await the call for renewed action. The operation of school, club, private and company-owned aircraft contributes to the movements.

A number of improvements have been made to the terminal building in recent years to enable it to cope with the growing IT traffic. The amount of cargo handled remains small, mail and parcels providing the main business.

Location and access: Situated 4 miles east of Exeter, 1 1/2 miles from M5 Junction 29.Turn off A30 at Clyst Honiton towards Farringdon and Aylesbeare. Car park has graduated charges with no free period. Devon Bus Service 356 runs between the airport and Belgrave Road (which is close to Exeter Bus and Coach Station). Services to Clyst Honiton run regularly from Exeter bus station, but this involves a walk of about a mile to the terminal along a narrow road without a footpath
Terminal: Includes a lounge, licensed bar, buffet, shop and conference room
Spectator facilities: A small viewing balcony is provided on the first floor with access from within the terminal. Its value as a photographic vantage point has diminished due to the provision of glass panels, although with care the

almost inevitable reflections can be avoided. Presumably this obstacle is intended to provide a measure of security. Similar precautions have been taken in the long-term car park where the existing 10ft-high chainlink fence has apparently been considered to give insufficient protection. This has been overcome by providing a second fence a few inches apart which effectively prevents photography through the wire. Strangely enough, alongside the access road the fence remains 4ft high.
Operators: Scheduled services by Air South West (Bandeirante, Navajo), Isles of Scilly Skybus (Islander, Twin Otter), Jersey European Airways (Friendship, Short SD3-60). *Charter and IT operators:* Air Europa (Boeing 737), Air Malta (Boeing 737), Air Transat (Boeing 757, TriStar), Air 2000 (Airbus A320, Boeing 757), British Midland (Boeing 737), Eurocypria (Airbus A320), Futura (Boeing 737), Oasis (MD83), Spanair (MD83), Viva Air (Boeing 737). *Cargo flights:* BAC Express (Short SD3-60), Channel Express (Herald), Jersey European Airways (Short SD3-60), Titan Airways (Short SD3-60)
Movements (1994): Total 51,745 (air transport 10,198/positioning 2,448/test & training 25,044/private 6,795/military 5,978). Total passengers 203,360
Runways: 08/26 (6,840ft/2,083m), 13/31 (4,393ft/1,339m)
Radio frequencies: 119.8MHz (Tower)/128.15MHz (Approach)
Telephone: Exeter (01392) 367433
Operated by: Exeter & Devon Airport Ltd

GATWICK

Although licensed for flying in 1930, Gatwick did not officially become an airport until June 1936. During the intervening years it became very popular with jockeys and the more influential racegoers because of its close proximity to the racecourse. Nevertheless, the airfield did little to reward its owners, causing it to change hands four times in almost as many years. By the mid-1930s the projected airport was under development, one of its design features being a very advanced terminal building which, because of its appearance, became known as the 'Beehive'. It incorporated an underground passageway to the adjacent railway station, again a novel feature in 1936 and an idea which 60 years later has been adopted by very few authorities. Gatwick was equipped with night flying aids and two hangars were constructed for the benefit of the

expected operators. One of these was British Airways, an airline formed on 1 October 1935 by the merger of Spartan Airways, United Airways and Hillman Airways, the last named being the successful private company based at Stapleford, Essex. Unfortunately, its new home suffered from waterlogging, a problem which resulted in the newcomer moving out after one year's residence.

A growing need for military personnel was responsible for the arrival of No 19 E&RFTS complete with Tiger Moths and Harts in October 1937. Additional buildings were then necessary especially since the unit was enlarged in the following year with a number of Magisters. At the beginning of the war the school was closed down and the civil flying ended. Blenheim squadrons were the main occupants of Gatwick until September 1940 when the station came under the wing of Army Co-Operation Command. Lysanders then became a familiar sight, outstaying the unsuccessful Tomahawk intended as its replacement. Mustangs took over in early 1942, taking part in several operations including the ill-fated Dieppe landings in August. With the formation of the Tactical Air Force in mid-1943, the Army Co-Operation Command was absorbed into it leaving Gatwick to be taken over by No 11 Group. Numerous Spitfire units passed through during the winter of 1943/44, flying on escort and attack missions. At the time of the D-Day landings much importance was placed on the activities of the photo-reconnaissance Mustang squadrons which had arrived just prior to the invasion. By August the operational units had moved out, their place taken by those involved in communications and support. Gradually Gatwick was run down as the size of the RAF shrank after the end of the war; the military finally relinquished its control on 31 August 1946.

As was customary in those days it was the Ministry of Civil Aviation that became responsible for the airfield. Despite its active role during the six hectic years no hard runways had been provided, a fact which did little to attract civilian operators. None the less, a number of companies took up residence in the period up to 1956, engaging in both charter and maintenance work. Already plans were being laid for Gatwick to become London's second airport, necessitating the dispersal of all

occupants while its reconstruction was under way. When opened two years later it possessed a single 7,000ft (2,133m) runway and a large apron over which a pier stretched from the brand-new terminal building. As before, this was connected to the railway, with British Rail rebuilding its station adjacent to the airport complex. On 9 June 1958 the opening ceremony was performed by The Queen and Prince Philip, the couple arriving in a Heron of the Royal Flight.

The formation of British United Airways in 1960 brought a considerable increase in activity at Gatwick, both scheduled and charter. A rapid upsurge of ITs in the 1960s saw a constant stream of airliners using the facilities, which by this time had been expanded to include two additional piers. To accommodate the larger types then coming into service, the runway was extended, first to 8,200ft (2,499m) in 1964 and later to 10,000ft (3,048m). Another major development began in the mid-1970s involving a vast terminal extension, multi-storey car park and a direct access road to the M23 motorway. Airside changes included additional parking areas and taxiways, while an emergency runway was laid parallel to the existing strip with completion in October 1985. Unfortunately, the separation distance was insufficient to permit its use for regular traffic.

Always a popular airport with the IT carriers, those offering scheduled services have also steadily grown in number. Home of British Caledonian, this operator made a considerable

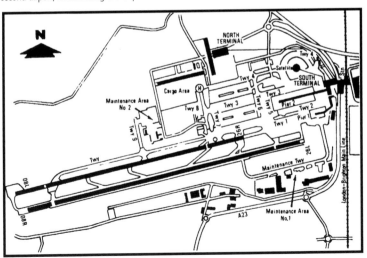

contribution to the movement statistics with both domestic, European and intercontinental flights until becoming a part of British Airways at the end of 1987. Dan-Air likewise was engaged in both types of operation, while the larger US airlines began to expand their networks to use Gatwick as the UK gateway in the 1980s. Such was the growth that plans were submitted for a second terminal on the north side of the airport. Connected to the original building by a transit system, the new complex opened in March 1988.

During the 1980s, Air Europe became a major force at the airport as its involvement in scheduled services became greater. Together with its IT work, the airline accounted for some 10% of the traffic, so when the company collapsed in March 1991 it had a marked effect on the figures. Fortunately it was only temporary because there were more than enough eager carriers willing to take over its commitments. The decision to give newcomers the opportunity to have access to Heathrow was responsible for a number of moves from Gatwick, but the void was soon filled by others keen to serve London whichever gateway was allocated. The growing shortage of runway space in the southeast of England resulted in a survey into the various options available, but it seems unlikely that a second runway will be built at Gatwick, although politicians have been known to reverse decisions!

The first phase of an £80 million redevelopment programme was opened in the spring of 1994. This produced a remodelled North Terminal international departure lounge complete with large balcony giving views over the airport. Three additional stands were also installed for BA European flights. Attention was then turned to the South Terminal which received a large shopping mall within the extended departure lounge, the new accommodation being opened in mid-1995. Long overdue improvements to the check-in area have produced a more spacious environment and less congestion in this busy section of the building.

Location and access: Situated 28 miles south of London on the A23 with a direct link to the M23 at Junction 9. Multi-storey and open car parks with graduated charges provided for both terminals. By rail the Gatwick Express runs non-stop between Victoria and the airport every 15min during the day, journey time 30min. On Sundays the trip takes 35min and during the night the trains run hourly with an elapsed time of up to 45min. Two Gatwick Link trains run

every hour between the airport and London Bridge with a journey time of 35min. Speedlink coaches connect Gatwick with Heathrow every 20min during the morning, half-hourly in the afternoon, with an hourly service in the evening. The trip takes about 60min depending on traffic congestion on the M25. Service 777 runs to Victoria coach station, while Jetlink routes run to Heathrow and Stansted airports. Further details from London Country on (01293) 507178. There are frequent local buses to both Crawley and Horley. Express coaches link various parts of the country with the London airports

Terminal: The large south building contains restaurants and snack bars on the catering level above the International arrivals hall. Shops and banks are also available within a large airside complex opened in mid-1995. Similar facilities are provided in the North Terminal

Spectator facilities: A gallery is situated on the roof of the South Terminal building giving good views of all movements, although some are rather distant. There is an admission charge. A refreshment buffet is available. As a photographic vantage point it has its limitations, although it is possible to secure shots of aircraft using the satellite and some of the nearer stands. Building work has further reduced the scope for photography of aircraft using the domestic stands. This restriction is a pity since Gatwick does handle airlines not to be seen elsewhere in the UK. The gallery area was refurbished in early 1996 and now contains a Comet nose section and Herald G-CEXP. There are no facilities provided in the North Terminal, neither is it possible to view through windows on the landside

Operators: Scheduled services by AB Shannon (One-Eleven), Air Baltic (Avro RJ70), Air Belfast (One-Eleven), Air France (Airbus A320, Boeing 737), Air Inter Europe (Airbus A320), Air Liberte (Boeing 737, MD83), Air Malta (Airbus A320, Boeing 737), Air Moldova (Tu-134), Air Seychelles (Boeing 767), Air UK (BAe 146), Air Zimbabwe (Boeing 767), Alitalia (DC-9, MD80), American Airlines (Boeing 767, MD11), Air 2000 (Boeing 757), BASE Regional Airlines (Jetstream 31), Belavia (Tu-134), Braathens (Boeing 737), British Airways (Boeing 737/747/767, DC-10), Brit Air (ATR42, SAAB SF340), Cameroon Airlines (Boeing 747), Centennial (MD83), CityFlyer Express (ATR42/72), Community Express (Jetstream 31, Short SD3-60), Continental Airlines (DC-10), Cyprus Airways (Airbus A310/A320), Delta Air Lines (MD11, TriStar), Deutsche BA (Boeing 737, Fokker 100, SAAB SF340), Emirates (Airbus

A310), Eurowings (ATR42/72), Estonia Air (Boeing 737), Finnair (DC-9, MD80), Garuda (MD11), GB Airways (Boeing 737), Iberia (MD87), Jersey European Airways (BAe 146, Friendship), L'Aeropostale (Boeing 737), Lauda Air (Boeing 737/767, Canadair RJ), Lufthansa (Avro RJ), Maersk Air (Boeing 737), Meridiana (BAe 146, DC-9), Northwest Airlines (Boeing 747, DC-10), Qatar Airways (Boeing 747), Regional Airlines (Bandeirante), Ryanair (Boeing 737), Philippine Airlines (Boeing 747), Royal Nepal Airlines (Airbus A310), Transavia (Boeing 737), Transwede (Fokker 100, MD80), Trans World Airlines (Boeing 747/767), Ukraine International (Boeing 737), Virgin Atlantic (Boeing 747), Yemenia (Airbus A310). *Charter and IT operators:* Adria Airlines (DC-9), Air Atlanta Iceland (Boeing 737), Air Club International (Airbus A310), Air Europa (Boeing 737), Air Jet (BAe 146), Air Ops (Airbus A300, TriStar), Airtours International (Airbus A320, Boeing 767), Air Transat (Boeing 757, TriStar), Air VIA (Tu-154B), Airworld (Airbus A320), Air 2000 (Airbus A320, Boeing 757), AJT Air International (Il-86), All Leisure (Airbus A320), American Trans Air (Boeing 757, TriStar), Austrian Airlines (MD80), Balkan (Tu-154B), Britannia Airways (Boeing 757/767), British World Airlines (BAe 146, One-Eleven), Caledonian Airways (Airbus A320, DC-10, TriStar), Canada 3000 (Boeing 757), El Al (Boeing 757), European Aviation Air Charter (One-Eleven), Excalibur Airways (Airbus A320, DC-10), GB Airways (Boeing 737), Istanbul Airlines (Boeing 737), Laker Airways (DC-10), Leisure International Airways (Airbus A320, Boeing 767), Monarch Airlines (Airbus A300/A320, Boeing 757), Oasis (MD80), Onur Air (Airbus A300/A320/A321), Pegasus (Boeing 737), Rich International (TriStar), Royal Air Maroc (Boeing 737), Royal Aviation (TriStar), Sabre Airways (Boeing 727/737), Spanair (MD80), Sunway (MD83), Tarom (One-Eleven), TEA Switzerland (Boeing 737), Transwede (MD87), Viva Air (Boeing 737). *Cargo flights:* Affretair (DC-8), Aurigny Air Services (Short SD3-60), Channel Express (Herald), DAS Air Cargo (Boeing 707,DC-10), DHL (Boeing 727), Gill Airways (ATR72), MK Airlines (DC-8), Trans Arabian Air Transport (Boeing 707)

Movements (1994): Total 191,646 (air transport 181,879/positioning 7,540/private 2,002). Total passengers 21,208,398

Runways: 08R/26L (10,363ft/3,159m), 08L/26R (8,415ft/2,565m used only in emergencies or if 08R/26L is closed, otherwise it serves as a taxiway)

Radio frequencies: 124.225MHz (Tower)/126.825MHz (Approach)/119.6MHz (Radar)

Telephone: Crawley (01293) 535353

Operated by: Gatwick Airport Ltd.

GLASGOW (ABBOTSINCH)

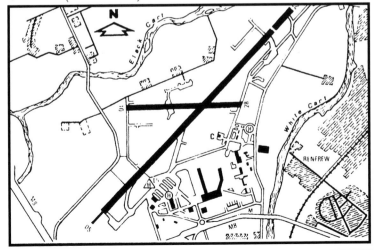

The airfield was established in 1932 for the RAF, becoming the home of No 602 (City of Glasgow) Squadron. Initially a light bomber unit equipped with Westland Wapitis, Hawker Hinds, Harts and later Hectors, its role changed during 1938 to that of a fighter squadron, receiving Spitfire Is by September 1939. The airfield remained under RAF control during the first three years of war, until in 1943 it was transferred to the Fleet Air Arm. As a Royal Naval Air Station it took the name of HMS *Sanderling*, remaining operational until the end of October 1963. Much of its activities involved the overhaul and repair of aircraft attached to carrier-based squadrons, its close proximity to Glasgow docks making it ideal for this purpose.

After its closure, the airfield was prepared for use as a civil airport under Glasgow Corporation's control, finally taking over from Renfrew in May 1966. The modern facilities were vastly superior to those of its overcrowded predecessor, immediately encouraging new airlines to include it in their route networks. It followed that during its first 10 operational years, passenger numbers and aircraft movements increased to such an extent that major surgery to the terminal became necessary. Under British Airports Authority since 1975, it was expected that the new extensions planned would cope with the annual figure of 3.5 million passengers forecast for the late 1980s.

One of the major highlights of 1975 was the start of the UK's first Shuttle service, operated by British Airways with Tridents between Glasgow and Heathrow. Nowadays the Boeing 757 has taken over the duties. The airport is in fact well served by airlines with a good choice of scheduled and IT flights available, both domestic and international. In late 1982 British Midland was awarded a licence to offer a London service using DC-9s in competition with the British Airways shuttle, which brought benefits to the travelling public. More expansion was begun in 1987 to provide a greater apron space and other improvements, but at the end of the decade work began on a major extension to the terminal building in order to accommodate the influx of transatlantic flights. By 1990 a new forecourt road system was in use while a new short-term car park had been opened. When Phase One of the £55 million project was opened in June 1992, it provided 70% more space for passengers, the increase encouraging more long-haul services to be introduced. The project was carried out without the need to close the terminal at any time, but such problems did not exist with Phase Two which included the provision of a brand-new international pier. Since this was built on a passenger-free area to the west of the terminal, apart from the task of joining it to the main building, disruption was kept to a minimum. The airport is now expected to handle 6.5 million passengers annually by the end of the decade, more than half of them flying on international services. In March 1994, a study by the Strathclyde Passenger Transport Executive confirmed the preferred route for a rail link between Paisley St James and the airport. The next stage will include feasibility studies to explore engineering and funding implications. Despite these impressive improvements, there was a set-back in 1994 when several of the long-haul carriers announced a reduction or suspension of services due to poor yields. Some 30 miles to the south, rival Prestwick has seen a resurgence of traffic both charter and scheduled, an interesting turn of events.

Location and access: Situated 10 miles west of Glasgow alongside the M8 at Junction 28. Car park charges graduated. There is a short-stay car park to the right of the terminal, with charges escalating rapidly after the basic period. An express coach service from the airport to the city centre (Central and Queen Street stations) operates every 20min taking about 20min for the journey. It then continues to Edinburgh where it arrives 1 1/2hr later. By rail from Glasgow Central to Paisley (Gilmour Street) takes 11min. A local bus runs every 10min to the airport from Paisley and less frequently from Renfrew

Terminal: All types of catering are available ranging from quick snacks to full meals. One buffet is open 24hr. There are two bars in the public section of the terminal plus another open 24hr in the international departure lounge. A number of shops offering a wide selection of goods have been provided during the various building extensions

Spectator facilities: The original excellent rooftop terrace has long been a victim of its constant need for expansion, with no alternative position provided for those either waving to departing friends and relatives, or others with an interest in the activities in general. However, it is understood that thought is being given to such a facility, but of course its priority will not be high. A few vantage points can be found around the perimeter, although the west-facing spots mean that mornings offer the best photographic opportunities

Operators: Scheduled services by Aer Lingus

(BAe 146, Fokker 50), Air Canada (Boeing 767), Air Malta (Boeing 737), Air UK (BAe 146, Fokker 100), British Airways (BAe ATP, Boeing 737/757), British Midland (BAe ATP, Boeing 737, Fokker 70, Jetstream 41), Brymon Airways (Dash Eight), Business Air (SAAB SF340), easyJet (Boeing 737), Icelandair (Boeing 737, Fokker 50), Loganair (Islander, Short SD3-60, Twin Otter), Manx Airlines (BAe ATP, Jetstream 41), Sabens/Delta Air Transport (Avro RJ85). *Charter and IT operators:* Adria (Airbus A320, DC-9), Air Club International (Boeing 747), Air Europa (Boeing 737), Air Malta (Boeing 737), Air Ops (TriStar), Airtours International (Boeing 757), Air Transat (Boeing 757, TriStar), Air VIA (Tu-154B), Air World (Airbus A320), Air 2000 (Airbus A320, Boeing 757), American Trans Air (Boeing 757, TriStar), AviaReps/Air Atlanta Icelandic (Boeing 737), Britannia Airways (Boeing 757), British Midland (Boeing 737),

Caledonian Airways (Airbus A320), Canada 3000 (Boeing 757), Centennial (MD83), Futura (Boeing 737), LOT (Boeing 737), Monarch Airlines (Boeing 757), Oasis (Airbus A310, MD83), Pegasus (Boeing 737), Royal Airlines (TriStar), Royal Air Maroc (Boeing 737), Spanair (MD83), Sunway (MD83), Viva Air (Boeing 737). *Cargo flights:* Atlantic Air Transport (Electra), Channel Express (Friendship, Herald), DHL (Convair 580)

Movements (1994): Total 95,482 (air transport 75,986/positioning 3,096/club 7,893/private 4,100/military 2,017).
Runways: 05/23 (8,720ft/2,658m), 10/28 (3,570ft/1,088m)
Radio frequencies: 118.8MHz (Tower)/119.1MHz (Approach)
Telephone: Glasgow (0141) 887 1111
Operated by: Glasgow Airport Ltd

GLOUCESTERSHIRE (STAVERTON)

The present airport at Staverton was opened in the summer of 1936, allowing the introduction of scheduled services by Railway Air Services on routes to Birmingham, Bristol, Southampton and Weston-super-Mare. The Air Ministry also took an interest, resulting in the erection of additional buildings to accommodate recruits passing through.

During the war Staverton was the home of several training schools, both advanced and elementary. It also housed the Rotol Flight Test Unit plus Folland and Flight Refuelling, both very active companies engaged in development work for the Air Ministry.

Peace brought a rapid reduction in Service activity, until the airfield was finally left to

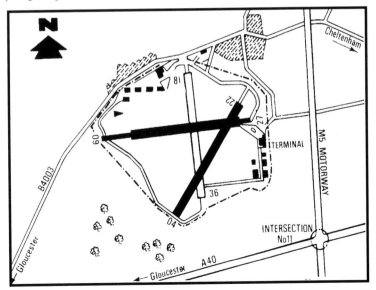

civilian interests. Murray Chown Aviation took over control in 1949, services to Jersey and Newquay commencing in 1951. At the end of the next year, the whole operation passed to Cambrian Airways. The Welsh carrier continued the Jersey service, although routeing it via Southampton for Customs purposes. It had the added benefit of providing a connection with the airline's Paris flight. By 1957, however, Cambrian had withdrawn, management of the airfield becoming the responsibility of Smiths Industries, a company associated with Staverton for many years.

Cambrian's successor was Derby Airways who carried on the now traditional Channel Islands operation. The airline's name change to British Midland did not affect the service, continuing until the end of the 1970 season. At this point Intra Airways took over ensuring that the airport's association with the Dakota and the Channel Islands continued until 1979 when after a route swap, Dan-Air became the licence holder, employing BAe 748s. In addition, the airline introduced a seasonal link with the Isle of Man with the same type of aircraft. This arrangement did not last long, with the Guernsey and Jersey routes passing to Guernsey Airlines in 1981, the Isle of Man being dropped from the schedules. The surviving services were also reduced to weekends only during 1982, a frequency subsequently maintained each summer until 1987. Thereafter the sorties were regarded as IT charter flights with the responsibility passing to Brymon and Capital. In 1990 the contract to carry the tour operator's clients to the Channel Islands was won by Celtic Air which proposed to use SD3-30s for the purpose. Problems with licensing meant that the task reverted to Capital, but following this carrier's demise at the end of June yet another change was necessary. This time Aurigny took over the movements with its SD3-60, an arrangement which continued until the end of the relatively short season. In the early 1990s there was an attempt to revive the scheduled services at Gloucestershire when Air Corbiere introduced regular links with Coventry and the

Channel Islands in 1992. The operation was continued during the next year, but in 1994 the operator changed to Orient Air and a sector to Waterford was added. Unfortunately, this carrier's career was short, quickly bringing an end to the flights, so during 1995 the traditional routes to Jersey and Guernsey were flown by Titan Airways using a Short SD3-60.

Staverton became the site for Skyfame, the first purely aviation museum set up by Mr Peter Thomas in 1963. However, in 1978 the Collection was forced to leave the airfield, fortunately many of the possessions finding a new home at Duxford.

Location and access: Situated off the B4063 Gloucester to Cheltenham road, the airport entrance being in Bamfurlong Lane. It is about half way between the two towns. The A40 and M5 Junction 11 are adjacent, although there is no direct link to the airport
Terminal: Contains small waiting area. Bar and refreshments available in nearby building
Spectator facilities: A grassed area equipped with seats alongside the entrance road gives a good viewing position. Good landing shots can be obtained when runway 27 is in use from the same vantage point. In both cases a telephoto lens is necessary for most types likely to be seen, although a standard lens will suffice for airliners landing on 27
Operators: Scheduled services suspended. *Charter and IT operators:* Titan Airways (Short SD3-60). Carriers can change year to year. Residents include the Cotswold Aero Club and privately-owned aircraft. A steady number of visiting machines contribute to the movements
Movements (1994): Total 70,485 (air transport 840/test & training 2,300/club 53,094/private 11,409). Total passengers 4,574
Runways: 09/27 (4,662ft/1,421m), 04/22 (3,189ft/972m)
Radio frequencies: 122.9MHz (Tower and Radar)/125.65MHz (Approach)
Telephone: Churchdown (01452) 857700
Operated by: Gloucestershire Airport Ltd

GUERNSEY

The island was much slower than neighbouring Jersey to accept civil aviation, since it was 1939 before the airport was opened at La Villiaze. After the German occupation, Channel Islands Airways resumed its operations, only to have them taken over by BEA in 1947. Despite some improvements during the military control period, the grass field was still often

waterlogged. No attempt was made to eliminate the problem until it became an economic necessity for BEA to withdraw its last Dakotas from service. In 1961 the Guernsey authorities reluctantly agreed to construct a runway, therefore permitting the regular use of Viscounts.

Although NLM employed a Fellowship on its

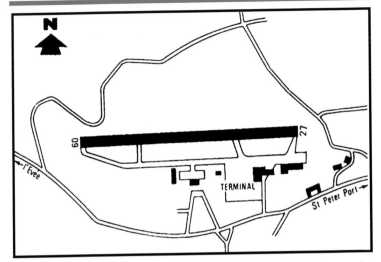

seasonal Amsterdam service for many years without undue comment from the local population, due to runway length and noise restrictions turboprops have always been favoured. However, a new era began in December 1987 when Air UK supplemented its Friendships with a BAe 146, a type which has since proved very popular. In a similar manner to Jersey, the airport closes at night, until the newspaper flights signal the start of a new day. By no means as busy as its more commercialised neighbour, Guernsey is served by many of the UK airlines direct, but in any case travel via Jersey is simple using Aurigny's frequent inter-island links.

The 1980 shuffle of routes following the British Airways decision to relinquish those that were unprofitable, left Guernsey in the hands of Air UK as the main operator to the UK. Both London airports became the preserve of Heralds, while the Southampton sector saw both Heralds and Friendships on the route. However, late in 1982 it was announced that the Guernsey-Gatwick route licence was to be transferred to Guernsey Airlines from the following April. A certain amount of political pressure was suspected, although the reasons given were that the equipment used was shabby. There were no comments made about the stability of the replacement SD3-30s compared with the Herald and Friendship after the changeover. With the sale of the airline to British Air Ferries, Viscounts and Heralds

became readily available to take over when necessary, the route prospering under the new management. In conjunction with its parent company, Guernsey Airlines steadily gained more licences to serve a large number of regional airports in the UK, linking them mainly on a seasonal basis to Guernsey and Jersey. In 1987 a Short SD3-60 joined the smaller 330s, all three supporting the Viscount on the busy summer routes. Despite the success of the business, there was a slack period during the winter months which caused a cash flow problem. In an effort to acquire more capital, Guernsey Airlines was sold to Aurigny Air Services with effect from 1 October. Initially it was not expected that there would be any obvious changes, the routes and equipment remaining unaltered.

However, it was not long before it was announced that the busy Southampton sector was to be dropped by the new owners. Naturally it produced a number of requests for the licence, with Air Atlantique eventually taking over in May 1988. One season with schedules proved sufficient for the company, so in the spring of the following year it was Jersey European that added the Southampton-Guernsey link to its growing network. Meanwhile Air UK had improved its image and in late 1986 introduced a Friendship 500 on the Heathrow sector, thereby offering another six seats on each flight. One year later the service was further upgraded by the arrival of the BAe

146, this type also taking over some of the Southampton work in due course. Unfortunately rising costs forced the airline to revert to the Friendship in order to maintain frequencies, a type joined by the more modern Fokker 50 in 1995.

In the autumn of 1989 Guernsey Airlines was merged into Air Europe Express leaving Aurigny to concentrate upon its well-established inter-island activities. The company added a Short SD3-60 to its fleet in May 1990 following the need for greater capacity on some routes, the repainting and overhaul work on the ex-Maersk specimen being carried out at Guernsey by Anglo-Normandy Aeroengineering. The collapse of Air Europe in early 1991 had its effect upon the island because it meant that Air Europe Express was also forced to cease operations. However, after two months or so it emerged as Euroworld, once again using the 360 for the restored Gatwick-Guernsey schedules. The airline changed its name to CityFlyer Express in February 1992, but began operating under the British Airways Express name after the signing of a five-year franchise agreement in August 1993. By the end of 1995 the carrier had disposed of its entire 360 fleet, which had gradually been replaced by ATR42s and 72s. There are still relatively few jet movements at Guernsey, with JEA's 146s employed on some of the London services and the occasional visit by one of British Midland's new Fokker 70s. A Lufthansa 737 also visits on summer Saturdays and is the only example of this type scheduled to appear.

Regular freight flights are operated by Channel Express carrying locally grown produce to the mainland in its Heralds, Friendships and Electras, while a considerable amount of traffic is generated by company, private and club aircraft.

Location and access: Situated 3 miles southwest of St Peter Port off Forest Road. Car park charges graduated. Regular bus services connect the airport with St Peter Port bus station taking about 25min for the journey
Terminal: Contains buffet, bar, lounge and shop
Spectator facilities: External stairs to the terminal roof which provides a very good vantage point for viewing and photography. Admission free. Other vantage points exist around the perimeter of the airport
Operators: Scheduled services by Air UK (Friendship, Fokker 50), Aurigny Air Services (Trislander, Short SD3-60), British Midland (BAe ATP, Fokker 70), Brymon Airways (Dash Eight), Channel Express (Friendship, Herald, Electra – freight), CityFlyer Express (ATR42/72), Crossair (SAAB SF340), Deutsche BA (SAAB SF340), Eurowings (ATR42/72), Gill Airways (ATR42), Jersey European (BAe 146, Friendship, Short SD3-60), KLM CityHopper (Fokker 50/70), Lufthansa CityLines (Boeing 737, Fokker 50), Manx (BAe ATP, Jetstream 41)
Movements (1994): Total 61,131 (air transport 39,850/positioning 2,103/club 4,827/private 4,723). Total passengers 822,918
Runway: 09/27 (4,800ft/1,463m)
Radio frequencies: 119.95MHz (Tower)/128.65MHz (Approach)/118.9MHz (Radar)
Telephone: Guernsey (01481) 37766
Operated by: States of Guernsey

HEATHROW

The site was earmarked for an airfield in 1928 by Fairey Aviation. It became operational two years later with the name of the Great West Aerodrome. Although taken over by the RAF during the war, it was not until May 1944 that work started on the reconstruction programme. The problems of securing funds in wartime for a civil venture dictated the design. It was supposedly intended for the use of Transport Command which meant that the designers were forced to adopt the familiar triangular pattern for the runways. It was so arranged that the airport could be expanded in stages, each causing as little interference as possible during construction.

Transport Command did take over for a short time in October 1945 when a number of officers and men arrived to ready the station for service. On 6 December the Lancastrian G-AGWG of British South American Airways landed prior to a proving flight to South America. This aircraft also made the first official flight from Heathrow on 1 January 1946 using the one completed runway.

Development continued from that point allowing the opening of the central terminal area in the mid-1950s, accessible via twin tunnels from the north side. The new complex gradually replaced the inferior temporary accommodation which had been used by long-haul passengers for many years.

Heathrow has become one of the world's leading international airports with over 90 airlines providing routes to all parts of the globe. The majority of the movements are those of scheduled services which carry some 50 million passengers annually. Executive aircraft are regular visitors, while the cargo facility opened in 1968 handles the considerable freight traffic generated by British Airways and many foreign airlines. As early as 1973 statistics were already giving a warning that passenger figures were steadily increasing each year, even allowing for the occasional hiccup due to the fuel crisis and recession. Overall the picture was one of growth with saturation point becoming closer. A new terminal was urgently required, but there was no more space in the centre island. Breaking away from this layout was the only solution, leading to the start of Terminal 4 in September 1981. Opened to traffic in April 1986, it now handles all BA's intercontinental services together with the airline's Paris, Amsterdam and Athens schedules. Also accommodated in the new premises are KLM, Air Malta and Air Lanka.

A long-standing policy was changed in 1991 when the authorities agreed to allow new carriers access to Heathrow. This relaxation of the rules came after American Airlines and United Airlines bought transatlantic routes from TWA and Pan Am respectively. A number of companies subsequently transferred their operations from Gatwick in the belief that

travellers would prefer using London's premier airport. Charter operators were also allowed back in limited numbers after an absence of over 20 years, with several tour operators offering Heathrow as an alternative departure point in their summer programmes. Needless to say, it did nothing to improve the congestion both land and airside, so investigations began into the feasibility of a fifth terminal and another runway to the north of the Bath Road. The latter proposal revived a scheme originally planned for the airport in the 1940s, but abandoned as unnecessary at the time. The same conclusion was reached some 50 years later, but it was agreed that the new terminal should be built to the west of the exisiting complex with independent access.

Location and access: Situated 14 miles west of central London with access direct from the M4 at Junction 4 or the A4 to the central area. Terminal 4 is alongside the A30 and can be reached from the M25. Each of the four terminals has its own short-term car park with rapidly escalating charges after the first two hours. One long-term car park is located on the eastern boundary. Courtesy buses shuttle backwards and forwards at frequent intervals, but the journey can be time consuming due to traffic delays either in, or approaching, the tunnel to the central area. Bearing in mind the amount of public transport available, it is often cheaper to leave the car outside the airport and

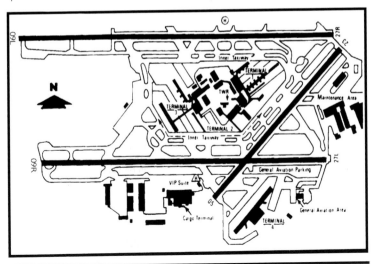

catch a bus or train. By using the Piccadilly Line from central London it is possible to complete the journey in about 50min. Trains stop at Hatton Cross on the boundary of the airport before travelling in a clockwise direction to Terminal 4 and Heathrow Central. The return trip to London takes the train around the remainder of the loop to Hatton Cross once again. A new rail link is under construction by BR so that fast trains can be operated from Paddington in a similar manner to those serving Gatwick from Victoria. Numerous local buses call at the airport central bus station to serve all four terminals. Coaches to most parts of the country either leave Heathrow or via a direct link with Victoria coach station. Express services are operated on this route and to Euston railway station. London Country has a direct Speedlink coach linking Gatwick and Heathrow every 20min, while Jetlink 747 has a similar purpose but also includes Luton in its itinerary. For full information telephone (0181) 745 5445

Terminals: All four have lounge areas, shops, restaurants, bars, buffets, bank and post offices. Terminal 4 has fewer facilities in the public area. Terminal 1 handles all British Airways (European Division) flights (except those to Paris, Amsterdam and Athens) plus all other UK airlines and Aer Lingus. As a result, congestion is not unknown in the building, particularly around the arrivals area. A major improvement scheme to enlarge the facilities on the northern side of Terminal 1 has provided more gatelounges and airbridge-equipped stands. Following the opening of Terminal 4 several other carriers using the central complex were relocated in order to achieve a better distribution of traffic in the terminals. As a result, Cyprus Airways, El Al, Finnair, Sabena, and South African Airways are handled by Terminal 1. The remaining European airlines use Terminal 2 with the exception of Icelandair, Lithuanian Airlines, SAS and Virgin, which are all allocated to Terminal 3

Spectator facilities: A terrace is provided over Terminal 2 with free admission. Although much smaller in area than in the past, it provides a good vantage point for viewing. Unfortunately, through the years the photographic opportunities have steadily declined as the number of new buildings and huts have grown along the front of the main building. Reasonable shots are possible of movements at Terminal 2's piers, while aircraft on the adjacent taxiways can also become good subjects. Sadly, the terrace gives the impression of being a temporary facility with little to attract the general public. It was reported that an alternative viewing area is under consideration by the BAA, but nothing definite has been decided

Operators: Scheduled services by Adria Airways (Airbus A320, DC-9, MD83), Aer Lingus (Boeing 737), Aeroflot (Airbus A310, Il-62/86, Tu-154), Aerolineas Argentinas (Boeing 747), Air Algerie (Boeing 727/737), Air Canada (Boeing 747/767), Air China (Boeing 747SP), Air France (Airbus A300/A320, Boeing 737, Canadair RJ, Fokker 70), Air India (Airbus A310, Boeing 747, TriStar), Air Lanka (Airbus A340), Air Malta (Airbus A310/A320, Boeing 737), Air Mauritius (Airbus A340), Air Namibia (Boeing 747SP), Air New Zealand (Boeing 747), Air Portugal (Airbus A310/A320/A340, Boeing 737), Air UK (Friendship, Fokker 50), Alitalia (Airbus A300/A321, DC-9, MD82), All Nippon (Boeing 747), Alliance (Boeing 747SP), Alyemda (Airbus A310), American Airlines (Boeing 767, MD11), Ariana Afghan Airlines (Boeing 727), Austrian Airlines (Airbus A310/A321/A340, MD80), Balkan (Airbus A320, Boeing 737), Bangladesh Biman (DC-10), British Airways (Airbus A320, Boeing 737/747/757/767/777, Concorde), British Mediterranean (Airbus A320), British Midland (Boeing 737, Fokker 70, Fokker 100), BWIA International (Airbus A340, TriStar), Brymon Airways (Dash Eight), Canadian Airlines International (Boeing 767, DC-10), Cathay Pacific (Boeing 747), Croatia Airlines (Boeing 737), Crossair (Avro RJ, SAAB 2000), CSA Czech Airlines (Boeing 737), Cyprus Airways (Airbus A310/A320), DHL/European Air Transport (Boeing 727), EgyptAir (Airbus A300/A320), El Al (Boeing 747/757/767), Emirates (Airbus A300), Ethiopian Airlines (Boeing 767), EVA Air (Boeing 747), Finnair (DC-9, MD80), Ghana Airways (DC-10), Gulf Air (Airbus A340, Boeing 767), Iberia (Airbus A320, Boeing 727/757, MD87), Icelandair (Boeing 737/757), Iran Air (Boeing 747), Istanbul Airlines (Boeing 737/757), Japan Airlines (Boeing 747), JAT (Boeing 737), Kenya Airways (Airbus A310), KLM (Boeing 737/767, Fokker 50, Fokker 70, Fokker 100), Korean Air (Boeing 747), Kuwait Airways (Airbus A300/A340, Boeing 747), Lithuanian Airlines (Boeing 737), LOT Polish Airlines (Boeing 737), Lufthansa (Airbus A300/A320/A321, Boeing 737), Luxair (Boeing 737), Malaysia Airlines (Boeing 747), Malev (Boeing 737), Manx Airlines (BAe ATP, BAe 146), Middle East Airlines (Airbus A310, Boeing 747), Olympic Airways (Airbus A300, Boeing 737), Pakistan International (Boeing 747), Qantas (Boeing 747), Royal Air Maroc (Boeing

737/757), Royal Brunei (Boeing 767), Royal Jordanian (Airbus A310), Sabena/Delta Air Transport (Avro RJ, Boeing 737, Dash Eight), Saudia (Boeing 747), SAS (Boeing 767, DC-9, MD80), Singapore Airlines (Boeing 747), South African Airways (Boeing 747), Sudan Airways (Airbus A310), Swissair (Airbus A320/A321, MD80), Syrian Arab Airlines (Boeing 727/747SP), TAT (Fokker 100), Tajik Air (Boeing 767), Tarom (Airbus A310, Boeing 737), Thai International (Boeing 747), Trans Mediterranean (Boeing 707), Tunis Air (Airbus A320, Boeing 727), THY Turkish Airlines (Airbus A310, Boeing 737), Turkmenistan Airlines (Boeing 737), United Airlines (Boeing 747/767/777), Uzbekistan Airways (Airbus A310), Varig (DC-10, MD11), Viasa (DC-10), Virgin Atlantic (Airbus A340, Boeing 747)

Movements (1994): Total 424,557 (air transport 411,608/positioning 4,680/private 6,248). Total passengers 51,720,996

Runways: 09R/27L (12,000ft/3,658m), 09L/27R (12,802ft/3,902m), 05/23 (6,450ft/1,966m)

Radio frequencies: 118.7MHz, 118.5MHz (Tower)/119.725MHz, 134.975MHz, 135.125MHz, 127.55MHz (Approach)

Telephone: London (0181) 759 4321

Operated by: Heathrow Airport Ltd

HUMBERSIDE (KIRMINGTON)

Construction work at Kirmington started in 1941, reaching a point when it was possible for a handover to Bomber Command in October 1942. During the first few months Wellingtons of No 150 Squadron were in residence, joined at the year's end by similar aircraft from No 140 Squadron. Sections of both merged in late January 1943 to form No 166 Squadron, this unit thereafter taking part in many of the war's major raids. In September that year, Lancasters were received, the type flown for the remainder of the squadron's existence. Over 27,000 tons of bombs were dropped by the unit, plus the laying of 333 tons of mines. After the last operational mission on 25 April 1944, when 24 of its aircraft attacked Berchtesgaden, the squadron was employed on supply runs and POW return ferry flights until disbanding in November 1945.

With its residents gone, Kirmington was quickly run down. After a spell on care and maintenance from February 1946, the site was allowed to be reclaimed as farmland. In the mid-1960s the Lindsey District Council considered the dilapidated airfield for possible redevelopment as the regional airport. Much reconstruction was necessary, but light aircraft began using the site again although even in 1968 there were only 236 movements. Gradually these increased, air-taxi companies such as Humber Airways helping things along.

It was March 1974 before the passenger terminal was completed and another year before Humberside Airport, as Kirmington was now known, was served by a scheduled flight. Air Anglia had earlier frequently used the airport for its air-taxi work, so it was not surprising that the airline created an outstation at Kirmington. The first route opened was to Amsterdam on 7 April 1975, followed later in the month by a weekend service to Jersey. Subsequently Air Anglia introduced links with Birmingham, Glasgow, Heathrow, Norwich and Teesside. With minor variations such services continued to the time of the formation of Air UK.

The steady expansion began to slow soon after the newly created airline took over the operations. The Birmingham and Teesside routes were dropped, while those to Glasgow and Heathrow were taken over by Eastern Airways initially employing DC-3s. However, it was not long before new equipment was introduced in the form of the Short SD3-30. The airline's main base was established at Humberside using the engineering facilities originally utilised by Air Anglia's outstationed Navajos.

In October 1982 the airline merged with Genair and Casair, although the combined fleet of SD3-30s and Bandeirantes became the responsibility of the Humberside headquarters. The benefits soon became evident with several new routes introduced in addition to expanding the Gatwick service into a direct operation on some timings. For a short time, therefore, Genair was Britain's leading commuter airline, but sadly it was a position that was relinquished in June 1984 when trading ceased. As usual licences were reallocated, some going to Air Ecosse with Air UK taking back the Humberside-Heathrow sector.

Meanwhile, this carrier continued to ply its Aberdeen, Amsterdam and Edinburgh routes which were the only others on offer at the time. After a brief period at Humberside, Air Ecosse left its services in the hands of Casair, until this company was forced to terminate its operations in March 1988. The airport's Danish link was re-established by Cimber Air in 1987, initially using an ATR42 for the regular runs until the smaller Nord 262 was found to be adequate for the fairly thin route to Esbjerg. In 1990 the airline decided to drop the schedule which was formally transferred to Newair, a Jetstream operator based at Copenhagen. In the meantime Humberside became the headquarters of Skyrover, which began a schedule in 1989 between the airport and Düsseldorf with the help of a leased Bandeirante. At the outset loads were very encouraging and soon prompted a change to the larger SD3-30. Unfortunately, as winter approached, so traffic rapidly declined to bring the inevitable suspension. It was intended to launch a new service to Esbjerg in the spring of 1990, but the licence was not forthcoming and in any case the route would not support two carriers.This belief was soon confirmed when Newair decided to drop the service from its network.

Once again Humberside was left with very few regular flights, but in mid-1994 there was fresh hope of a revival. Newcomer Euro Direct selected Humberside as one of the regional airports it considered suitable for the development of scheduled services. A number of domestic and international routes were either launched or planned using Jetstream 31s or ATPs. Market research had shown that there was a large number of potential travellers in the catchment area, but sadly, in reality few seemed willing to support the new venture. It meant that Euro Direct quickly began to drop uneconomic services, until eventually the airline itself was forced to end its brief but eventful career. An associate company, Euro Direct Belgium, had earlier introduced a link between its base at Kortrijk and Stansted, which was actually one of the few to attract reasonable loads. It was therefore a set-back for the carrier when its parent ceased operations, but after a few weeks, the company resumed flying as an independent, this time using Humberside as the UK gateway. A further change came at the end of 1995 when the route was added to SABENA's network. although still flown by Euro Direct's Jetstream 31. City Air Bus also attempted to offer scheduled services at the end of 1994, in this case linking the airport with London City using Dornier 228s for the frequent trips. A route to Cardiff was due to be introduced, but the airline abruptly terminated its short-lived commercial activities before the inaugural flight was completed.

For many years Humberside did not enjoy a great deal of IT charter traffic, although such types as Caravelles, Boeing 737s and Viscounts made occasional appearances. The situation

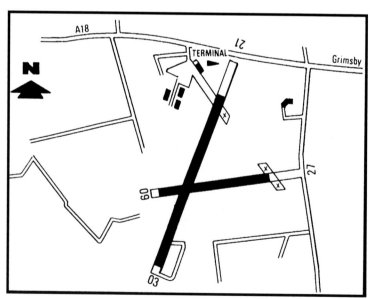

improved after a terminal extension in 1987, while lengthening the runway and enhancing the lighting and navigation aids in the early 1990s encouraged tour operators to offer a greater choice of destinations. It meant that holidaymakers were no longer forced to travel to Leeds, East Midlands or Manchester for their flights to the sun. Further expansion was announced for 1995 which included an expanded arrivals hall and refreshment area in the terminal.

Location and access: Situated 15 miles east of Scunthorpe alongside A18. The M180 motorway Junction 5 is 3 miles from the airport connecting with the direct link to the Humber Bridge. Via this route Hull is about 20 miles distant. Car park has graduated charges. A bus runs from Scunthorpe and Grimsby taking 45min approximately from each at two hourly intervals
Terminal: The single-storey building contains buffet, bar, shop and lounge area
Spectator facilities: The restaurant has been sited to overlook the apron so providing an improved viewing area. It is also possible to obtain photographs through the security fence bordering the northern side of the apron, with afternoons presenting better opportunities on sunny days
Operators: Scheduled services by Air UK (Friendship, Fokker 50), Euro Direct Belgium /SABENA (Jetstream 31). *Charter and IT operators:* Air Malta (Boeing 737), Airtours International (Airbus A320), Britannia Airways (Boeing 757), Futura (Boeing 737), Spanair (MD83), Sunway (MD83)
Movements: (1994): Total 35,633 (air transport 12,018/positioning 2,087/test & training 3,846/club 14,191/private 1,978). Total passengers 262,893
Runways: 03/21 (7,316ft/2,230m), 9/27 (3,458ft/1,054m)
Radio frequencies: 124.675MHz (Tower and Approach)/123.15MHz (Radar)
Telephone: Barnetby (01652) 688456
Operated by: Humberside International Airport Ltd

INVERNESS (DALCROSS)

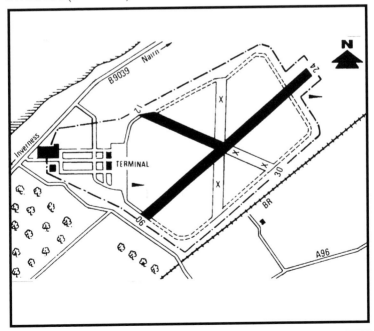

Civil flying was carried out prewar from a small field beside the Moray Firth about one mile north of Inverness. The present airport at Dalcross was built for the RAF at the beginning of the war, for most of its early life serving as a base for an advanced flying training and gunnery school. It passed to Fighter Command towards the end of the war, becoming a civil airfield in 1947. Nevertheless it reverted to military training again in the early 1950s when the Oxfords of 8 FTS arrived as a result of the demand for pilots in the expanding RAF.

Scheduled services have been continued through the years by BEA, British Airways and more recently Loganair; movements having increased considerably thanks to the oil business requirements. Runway improvements during 1974 enabled British Airways to include One-Elevens and Tridents on some of the London timings. The route was relinquished by the airline in 1983 whereupon it was taken over by Dan-Air until its demise in 1992, at which point the sector reverted to the flag carrier. A terminal extension was carried out in 1979 to deal with the upsurge in traffic. At the same time the opportunity was taken to run a campaign to encourage greater use of the airport by airlines and tour operators alike.

Locally-based clubs, training aircraft from Perth and privately-owned machines also use the facilities. Visits are also made by larger transports such as foreign registered Friendships from time to time. Military aircraft are not an uncommon sight.

Location and access: Situated 8 miles northeast of Inverness off A96 from which it is signposted. Car park charges graduated. Coaches to Inverness connect with flights
Terminal: Single-storey building containing bar, buffet and small lounge area
Spectator facilities: None provided. Good views can be obtained from within the terminal, although photography is impeded by the tinted glass. It is possible to find other vantage points for this purpose
Operators: Scheduled services by British Airways (BAe ATP, Boeing 737), Loganair (Short SD3-60). *Cargo flights:* Business Air (SAAB SF340)
Movements (1994): Total 23,923 (air transport 6,988/positioning 2,949/test & training 1,656/club 11,336). Total passengers 280,274
Runways: 06/24 (6,191ft/1,887m), 12/30 (2,296ft/700m). Taxiways not in use apart from those from the apron to runways 06 and 12
Radio frequency: 122.6MHz (Tower and Approach)
Telephone: Inverness (01463) 232471
Operated by: Highlands and Islands Airports Ltd

IPSWICH

Created at a time when airfield provision was becoming fashionable, Ipswich was officially opened by the Prince of Wales on 26 June 1930. Used initially by the Suffolk Aero Club, the site was taken over by the Whitney Straight Corporation in 1936. Its aircraft were used for exercises in both the Army and Observer Corps until the war, joined in 1938 by a detachment of the Civil Air Guard. As a satellite for nearby Wattisham, Ipswich quickly received some of the station's Blenheim IVs as the squadrons dispersed in September 1939. Generally they returned home when needed for operations, but a few sorties were flown from their temporary home in February/March 1941. A change of owner took place in the spring of 1942 when Martlesham Heath took control, leading to a succession of short visits by Spitfire units.

Promotion came in March 1943 when Ipswich was elevated to full RAF Station status, but its involvement with operations ended. Instead it became the base for a motley collection of target-towing flights equipped with Henleys and Martinets. For much of the time the machines ambled along the Essex and Suffolk coast inviting the naval gunners around the Harwich area to demonstrate their skills, a pursuit which continued until 1945. At various times the Army installed some of its Auster IIIs on the airfield, but these departed at the time of D-Day in 1944. Ipswich had little to offer the peacetime RAF, so the Air Ministry quickly put it on a care and maintenance basis in August 1945, before releasing the site for civil flying during the following year.

Club and private flying was resumed, there being little to attract the attentions of commercial operators at that stage. At Southend, East Anglian Flying Services (EAFS) was steadily expanding its charter activities during the late 1940s, supplementing this business with a few seasonal schedules to Ostend and Jersey. In 1953 the company received authority to launch an Ipswich-Southend-Rochester-Shoreham-Jersey service, while an Ipswich-Southend-Calais route was approved later that year. East Anglian decided to lease Ipswich Airport from the Corporation from 1 April 1954, the number of destinations on offer increasing considerably as a result of the connections available at Southend. Rapides had been used exclusively until the mid-1950s, but the need for more capacity then brought some Doves into the fleet. Both types became regular sights at Ipswich where the airline also established the East Anglian Flying Club equipped with Austers and Tiger Moths.

By the 1960s larger types were in service, DC-3s operating some of the flights from the airport. They carried the livery of Channel Airways, the name officially adopted by EAFS on 29 October 1962, although the title had been used by the company for many years. Modernisation programmes in the mid-1960s saw the arrival of HS 748s to replace the DC-3s, the new type taking over the schedules from Ipswich. However, it was not for long. Two landing accidents at Portsmouth on 15 August 1967 hastened the end of the type's scheduled operations from grass-covered airports, although Herons and Doves continued to visit the Suffolk field to provide feeder links with Southend. Equipped with Viscounts, One-Elevens, Tridents and Comets at the end of the decade, Channel had little interest in Ipswich with its limited potential. Therefore when the carrier ceased trading in February 1972 it had little effect on the airport. Herons were still to be seen, but in the colours of Peters Aviation based at Norwich. No one it seemed was willing to offer schedules, presumably on the assumption that travellers were prepared to make use of the facilities available at Norwich and Stansted, both some distance from Ipswich.

For the next 14 years or so the airport was deprived of regular flights, the terminal building settling down to deteriorate quietly. In the meantime industrial development in the area had greatly increased the demand for air links, so it was with this in mind that Suckling Airways was formed. Originally licences were sought to serve both Amsterdam and Rotterdam on a triangular course using a Twin Otter, but with the application modified to include Manchester, this type became unsuitable. Instead a Dornier 228 was acquired to ply the routes awarded by the CAA, the inaugural sortie to Schiphol taking place on 15 May 1986. Although Rotterdam was not included in the initial programme, it was intended to add this important centre to the company's network as soon as feasible. Such a service certainly seemed likely to succeed in view of the void left by the demise of Holland Aero Lines early in 1987. However, Suckling decided against the expansion to concentrate its resources on its existing routes. Normally Ipswich has an excellent, well drained

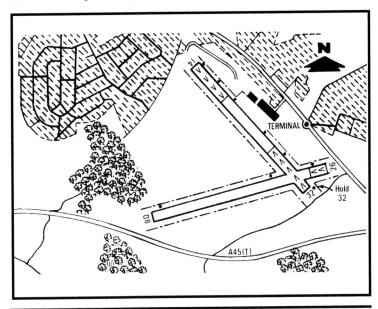

grass surface and at the time was one of few to accommodate scheduled services without the benefit of a hard runway. Unfortunately the persistent downpours during the winter of 1987/88 tested its ability to accommodate the regular movements of the Dornier which steadily introduced a network of ruts and indentations. The situation quickly deteriorated until it became necessary to close the airport. Suckling managed to transfer its terminal to RAF Wattisham as a temporary expedient, but intended to return to Ipswich as soon as possible.

This proved more difficult than expected because the airfield's operator refused permission in view of the damage likely to be caused by the 228's narrow-track undercarriage. In the long term a hard runway was the only solution, but the prospects for this were not good. A new operating base was therefore necessary for Suckling, so after evaluating the various options, the airline began flying from Cambridge on 18 July 1988.

Ipswich was therefore deprived of its popular scheduled services with little likelihood of ever enjoying the convenience again. Indeed the very existence of the field was placed in danger of extinction by 1994 following a decision by its Council owners to redevelop the entire site. In the event there was no action taken, so the airport continued to be active at the beginning of 1996. A new charter company known as Hawk Air moved in during 1995 which seemed to indicate confidence in the site's future. A number of interesting types often pass through after their arrival by sea at nearby Felixstowe. If Ipswich is eventually closed, it now seems unlikely that Wattisham will be available as a replacement following the arrival of the Army at the former RAF base.

Location and access: Situated 2 miles southeast of Ipswich to the north of the A14. A bus links the town centre with the airport entrance every 20min, while a circular route visits hourly

Terminal: Bar and coffee lounge. Refreshments available

Spectator facilities: A grass enclosure is provided in front of the terminal affording excellent views of all movements

Operators: Scheduled services suspended

Movements (1994): Not available

Runways: 08/26 (3,690ft/1,125m grass) 14/32 (3,379ft/1,030m grass)

Radio frequency: 118.325MHz (Tower and Approach)

Telephone: Ipswich (01473) 720111

Operated by: Ipswich Borough Council

ISLE OF MAN (RONALDSWAY)

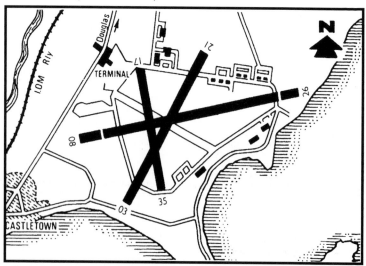

Services to the Isle of Man started in the mid-1930s, flown by several carriers from the mainland. The commercial link with Liverpool was maintained throughout the war although Ronaldsway was used extensively by the RAF and FAA particularly for training purposes. The airfield was returned to the civil authorities in 1946.

BEA took over the passenger services in the following year, which by this time included Liverpool, Blackpool, Carlisle and Glasgow. The network was further expanded by several independents in 1948 working under the Associate Agreement scheme.

For many years the routes remained generally unchanged although they passed through the hands of many different carriers. British Airways continued to serve the island on a much reduced scale from only London and Manchester until March 1980 when the carrier discontinued many of its domestic routes. As a result, the links with Heathrow, Liverpool and Belfast joined the British Midland network, while Air UK took on the Blackpool, Manchester, Glasgow and Dublin sectors on an all-year-round basis, with seasonal flights to Jersey, Edinburgh and Leeds. Dan-Air also acquired a share, providing seasonal services between Ronaldsway and Newcastle, East Midlands, Bristol and Gatwick.

It was announced in mid-1982 that a new carrier, Manx Airlines, was to take over the operation of all the Isle of Man services currently flown by Air UK and British Midland. Since it was a joint venture both airlines transferred aircraft to the newcomer to allow operations to begin on 1 November 1982. With a relatively small but effective fleet, Manx quickly gained the support of the islanders at the expense of the sea ferries. Although the company's main routes are those to Heathrow and Liverpool, there are others maintained throughout the year plus those of a seasonal nature. Almost all of the routes to the island are now flown by Manx, the exceptions being those in the hands of Jersey European. During 1987 there were indications that a new airline was being set up at Ronaldsway to offer some competition to Manx, but it did not materialise.

Location and access: Situated 7 miles southwest of Douglas near Castletown. Car park charges gently graduated. The Isle of Man Passenger Transport Board operates regular services connecting the airport with Castletown, Douglas, Port Erin and Port St Mary
Terminal: Contains buffet, bar, restaurant and waiting area
Spectator facilities: A grass area is available on the south side of the terminal and viewing is also possible from within the building
Operators: Jersey European Airways (BAe 146, Friendship, Short SD3-60), Manx Airlines (BAe 146, BAe ATP, Jetstream 31/41). Cargo flights: Emerald Airways (HS 748), Gill Airways (Short SD3-60)
Movements (1994): 39,991 (air transport 17,516/positioning 1,469/test & training 1,543/club 10,990/private 7,823). Total passengers 532,526
Runways: 03/21 (4,153ft/1,266m), 08/26 (5,750ft/1,753m), 17/35 (2,962ft/903m)
Radio frequencies: 118.9MHz (Tower)/120.85MHz (Approach)
Telephone: Castletown (01624) 823311
Operated by: Isle of Man Government Department of Highways, Ports and Properties

JERSEY

The present airport was opened on 10 March 1937, replacing the beach landing area at St Aubin's Bay. Numerous scheduled services were operated to the UK and France by Channel Island Airways up to the German occupation in June 1940, after which time the Luftwaffe made use of the facilities.

In 1945 the prewar carrier resumed operations, but after two years BEA took over the routes. Soon the growing size and number of aircraft using the airport necessitated the provision of a hard runway in 1951/52. This has since been extended at regular intervals to keep pace with the traffic increases as such types as the Viscount, Vanguard and One-Eleven were introduced. The terminal has also been progressively extended to accommodate the corresponding upsurge in passengers.

The island has also been served by a variety of independent carriers since 1951, including the locally based Jersey Airlines until its absorption into British United (CI) Airways, later British Island Airways, in 1967. Jersey became the headquarters of Intra Airways (now Jersey European) in 1969, scheduled services slowly building up from 1971. Regular inter-island services have been provided by Aurigny Air Services since 1968, the airline later adding Cherbourg to its network.

In 1980 British Airways closed its

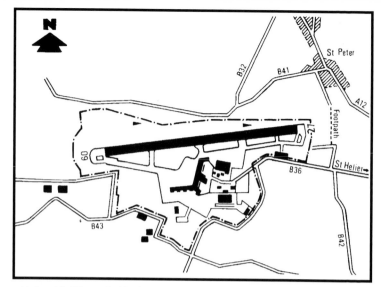

outstationed facilities on the island and with it most of the links with the UK. The relinquished routes were taken over by the independent carriers Air UK, Jersey European, Dan-Air and British Midland. In due course further reshuffling within this group allowed a few more airlines the opportunity to fly to Jersey.

Of these British Air Ferries and Guernsey Airlines flew both charters and schedules from 14 or so UK regional airports, mainly during the summer season. Jersey tourist authorities maintain a tight control on the number of flights allowed into the island because obviously there is a limit to the number of beds available for visitors at any one time. Nevertheless, on summer weekends there is a constant stream of movements of which a good proportion is IT charter traffic. Prices also play a part in limiting the number of travellers visiting the island because neither accommodation nor air fares are cheap. The airport returns to normal on weekdays with usually only a relatively few scheduled services in evidence.

One item that cannot be controlled is the weather. Jersey can suddenly be afflicted by sea fog or low cloud making operations impossible. Enormous backlogs can quickly build up in the peak season necessitating extra flights and rearranged schedules once there is a clearance.

While the amount of freight handled at the airport continues to grow, there are no plans to increase the size of the modest cargo terminal.

Newspapers are flown to the island by Channel Express which is also responsible for the transport of the flower crop back to the mainland.

The considerable number of movements at Jersey include many light aircraft. The local flying club operates its own machines, but the airport also attracts the attention of many visitors, particularly at weekends during the summer months. Every year, usually on the first weekend in May, an international rally is held to commemorate the liberation in 1945.

Location and access: Situated 5 miles northwest of St Helier off the A12 Beaumont to St Peter road. The airport is adequately signposted. Car park charges graduated. A JMT bus runs every 20min between the airport and Weighbridge Bus Station near the harbour in St Helier. Journey time is about 25min
Terminal: Contains restaurant, buffet, bar, lounge and shop
Spectator facilities: A set of external stairs on the right hand side of the terminal building leads to two small areas of roof which are excellent vantage points for viewing and photography. Admission is free. Other very good locations exist towards the ends of the runway and along the northern perimeter. Light aircraft park on the grass adjacent to the airport access road from where many can be photographed over the fence

Operators: Scheduled services by Aer Lingus (Fokker 50), Air UK (BAe 146, Friendship, Fokker 50, Fokker 100), Aurigny Air Services (Short SD3-60, Trislander), British Airways (BAe ATP, Boeing 737), British Midland (BAe ATP, Fokker 70, Fokker 100, Jetstream 41), Brymon Airways (Dash Eight), CityFlyer Express (ATR42/72), Crossair (SAAB SF340), Deutsche BA (SAAB SF340), Eurowings (ATR42/72), Gill Airways (ATR42/72, Short SD3-60), Jersey European Airways (BAe 146, Friendship, Short SD3-60), KLM CityHopper (Fokker 50/Fokker 70), Lufthansa (Boeing 737), Lufthansa CityLine (Fokker 50), Manx Airlines (BAe 146, BAe ATP, Jetstream 41). *Charter and IT operators:* Atlanta Iceland (Boeing 737), Braathens (Boeing 737), British Airways (BAe ATP), Brymon Airways (Dash Eight), Business Air (SAAB SF340), European Aviation Air Charter (One-Eleven), Finnair (MD87), Leisure International (Airbus A320) Maersk Air Ltd (One-Eleven), Manx Airlines (BAe ATP), Titan Airways (ATR42, BAe 146/Short SD3-60), Transwede (Fokker 100, MD83). *Cargo flights:* Aurigny Air Services (Short SD3-60), Channel Express (Electra, Friendship, Herald)

Movements (1994): Total 81,308 (air transport 49,018/club 14,296/private 15,564). Total passengers 1,671,786

Runway: 09/27 (5,597ft/1,706m)

Radio frequencies: 119.45MHz (Tower)/120.3MHz, 118.55MHz (Approach)

Telephone: Jersey (01534) 46111

Operated by: States of Jersey

KENT INTERNATIONAL (MANSTON)

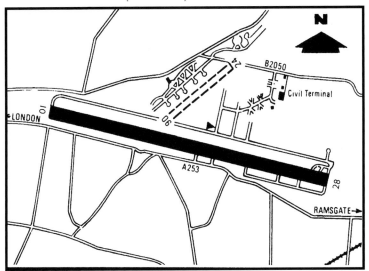

Flying began from the site in 1915, albeit on a fairly limited scale. During the following year the Royal Naval Air Service expanded the facilities, using the airfield mainly for training purposes. Following the formation of the RAF in April 1918 Manston was earmarked as a permanent base. It brought the provision of new buildings to house the influx of more personnel, although the main activities on the airfield were still predominantly concerned with training in some guise.

Its geographical position helped to determine Manston's role at the start of World War 2, which was that of an advanced fighter station, with all the non-operational units dispersed elsewhere, Fighter Command took control in November 1939 thereafter moving its squadrons in and out of what was to become the front line. Subjected to many intensive Luftwaffe attacks, there were times when the airfield was unusable, but by 1941 Manston was able to take a more aggressive role.

Although still a grass airfield, extensions had lengthened the runways which were frequently used by returning aircraft badly damaged in combat. Eventually it was decided to construct a long and wide runway designed specifically to aid the safe arrival of stricken bombers and fighters. Work started in June 1943, operational flying continuing from a temporary grass strip. Despite the size of the task, the contractor expedited the completion of the work to enable the new runway to come into use in April 1944. It was also one of the few in the UK to be equipped with FIDO to permit landings in the densest of fog, a facility which saved many lives before the end of the war.

Transport Command assumed control of Manston in April 1946, Dakotas becoming the main occupants although both freight and personnel also staged through on their way overseas. In 1950 the station reverted to Fighter Command, but only to act as a caretaker pending the arrival of the USAF in July 1950. Various fighter wings then spent periods at Manston, joined at times by search and rescue aircraft. During the eight years or so that the airfield was occupied by the Americans, several construction projects were completed including a batch of new hardstandings.

Under care and maintenance for a short time, Manston became the base for Silver City in April 1959, a move made necessary by the closure of Blackbushe. Using Handley Page Hermes, the company flew regular services between Kent and Le Touquet plus an intensive programme of ITs. This activity continued until the spring of 1962 when the airline became a part of the new Gatwick-based British United Airways. Its place at Manston was filled by Air Ferry equipped with Vikings and a DC-4, operations starting on 30 March 1963. In conjunction with Leroy Tours, the airline began to fly ITs to all parts of Europe. A scheduled licence was acquired for a Manston-Verona link, but his was never launched. Taken over by the Air Holdings group in late 1964, the next year saw the carrier operating vehicle ferry services from Manston to Calais, Le Touquet, Ostend and Rotterdam using Bristol Freighters leased from British United. Two DC-6s arrived at the end of 1965, remaining in service until the airline's closedown at the end of October 1968.

Another company closely associated with Manston was Invicta Airways. Formed in November 1964, this airline was also involved in IT flights which were started on 20 March 1965 with a trip to Basle. Such was the carrier's success that three DC-4s and two Vikings joined the three-strong fleet for the company's second

season. Invicta was also awarded a scheduled licence to link Manston with Ostend, an enterprise launched in May 1966. Three years later a merger with British Midland ended the airline's passenger activities from Manston, but after a short time a new company emerged to resume work at the base. This time Invicta Air Cargo concentrated on freight movements, a pursuit continued until 1971 when passenger charters were restarted with Vanguards. However, most of this flying was carried out from Luton with only an occasional charter operating from Manston, freight remaining the principal occupation at the airport until the demise of Invicta in 1981.

Throughout the period a military presence had continued, Chipmunks and rescue helicopters becoming the normal residents, although its role as a diversion airfield was maintained. Manston is also regularly used by RAF and foreign air forces' aircraft on training details or in transit.

In 1982 the civil operation was acquired by Seaborne Aviation, a company intent on expanding the airport's business generally. While executive and privately-owned aircraft use the facilities, there has been little interest shown by airlines. However, British Air Ferries introduced a seasonal Saturdays flight to Jersey in 1984 using one of its Viscounts, a service not only repeated in the following years, but expanded in 1986 to offer direct links with Guernsey also.

Unfortunately BAF was too involved in its own efforts to survive in 1988, so the series was flown by Dan-Air 748s instead. There was another change for the next season when Brymon became the contracted carrier for the weekly Channel Islands routes, but in 1990 Capital took over the responsibility for the Guernsey operation by routeing its 360 via Lydd both inbound and outbound. This arrangement did not last for very long due to the airline's collapse at the end of June, so thereafter passengers were carried on Brymon's Jersey flight.

Since the early 1970s, IT activities from Manston have not been particularly numerous, but during the 1980s flights to both Yugoslavia and Majorca were available, albeit on a modest scale. Both Adria and Aviogenex operated the former with Dan-Air positioning a One-Eleven from and to Gatwick for the weekly visit to Palma.

A regular cargo service was begun by Aeron International in 1986, but with the sale of its CL-44s two years later, the airline terminated the visits. In 1990 another freight run was introduced by Tampa Colombia involving a DC-8 arriving every Saturday from Bogota with flowers and fruit.

Prior to 1989 the terminal facilities were not very impressive, but this all changed with the official opening of a brand-new building in October. A simple but attractive design was chosen which unusually does not resemble a DIY centre. Its spacious interior is ample to cope with existing traffic, but there is room to expand when the need arises.

Even before this development, the title Kent International had been adopted to improve its chances of attracting a greater number of movements, particularly in view of the rapidly growing congestion at other southeast airports. During the summer of 1990 KIA was one of several named as possible candidates to relieve this situation, a duty it could undertake without massive runway construction. Road access is the main problem, but this could be rectified fairly easily. Whether operators could be encouraged to move so far from London is another question. As is often the case with these political affairs, no decision was taken in the first half of the 1990s, but instead the airport has become a popular gateway for eastern European cargo aircraft. Both IL-76s and An-12s are regular visitors and have been found invaluable for lifting heavy consignments destined for Russia and the neighbouring states. Even passenger ITs flown have employed Tu-134s or Yak-42s, the latter proving popular with both passengers and tour operators. Bulgarian independent, Air Sofia, has a base at KIA, using an An-12 for *ad hoc* freight charters. The airport's revival has been largely due to the easier market conditions and the creation of hundreds of small carriers in the former Soviet Union, all anxious to share in the new-found freedom. Even with no more major expansion, KIA seems set for a profitable and useful future.

Location and access: Situated 4 miles west-northwest of Ramsgate. Entrance is on B2050 via A253. It is now signposted as Kent International. Long- and short-term car parks, the latter offering the first 4hrs free. An East Kent bus runs irregularly from Ramsgate Harbour taking about 20min for the journey
Terminal: Single-storey building contains lounge, buffet and bar
Spectator facilities: None provided. A good view of the apron is possible from the clean buffet windows through which photographs can be taken. Almost the same scene can be observed from the long-term car park adjacent to the terminal, but here the familiar chainlink fence provides the handicap. Nevertheless, photographs are not too difficult to obtain, especially using a 200mm lens. Located opposite the military entrance is a small collection of RAF aircraft
Operators: Scheduled services suspended. *Charter and IT operators:* Air Atlanta Iceland (Boeing 737), Eurocypria (Airbus A320), LatCharter (Tu-134B, Yak-42), Titan Airways (Short SD3-60). *Freight flights:* Air Sofia (An-12), Atlant Soyuz (Il-76), Inversia (Il-76), Moscow Airways (Il-76), North East Cargo Airlines (An-12, Il-76), Penza (An-12), Sayakhat (Il-76), Trans Avia Export (Il-76), Turkmenistan Airways (Il-76)
Movements (1994): Total 14,131 (air transport 298/positioning 597/club 10,946/private 2,230). Total passengers 6,510
Runways: 10/28 (9,029ft/2,752m), 06/24 (2,598ft/792m grass)
Radio frequencies: 119.275MHz (Tower)/126.35MHz (Approach)
Telephone: Manston (01843) 823333
Owned by: Ministry of Defence. Civil operator Kent International Airport Ltd

LAND'S END (ST JUST)

Prior to the mid-1930s travellers to the Scilly Isles were forced to entrust themselves to the ship which regularly linked the islands with Penzance. Always a lively stretch of water, the 4hr journey was something of an endurance test. There was obviously scope for an air service, but it was 1935 before proving flights were introduced using some land between Sennen and St Just for the mainland terminal. Needless to say, the enterprise met with approval, especially since the trip over the water was completed in 20min. As a result,

Land's End Airport was opened in September 1937 to handle the scheduled service offered by Channel Air Ferries. Later this carrier became a part of the Great Western & Southern Airlines (GW&S) which not only continued the operation but increased the frequency, using Dragons G-ACPY and G-ADDI. In May 1939 the airline added Plymouth and Bristol to the new route, while Western Airways began a new service linking St Just with Newquay, Barnstaple and Swansea.

At the outbreak of war all commercial flying

was suspended, but it was not long before it was realised that the islands needed regular communications in view of their strategic importance, so the Dragons resumed work. One aircraft was delegated for exercises with the Army, leaving the second (G-ACPY) to cope with the return trips to St Mary's, the number varying with the demand. Unfortunately the faithful Dragon was lost *en route* to St Just on 3 June 1941, believed to be the victim of a Ju88 attack. Once more the service was suspended, to be temporarily reinstated in the autumn. On 4 November, Land's End airfield was closed down completely until May 1945 when the GW&S restarted the schedules, but this time using Rapides.

Postwar policy meant that the carrier became a part of the newly-formed British European Airways, although it was 1 February 1947 before the latter was in a position to take over all the domestic routes and fleets. In the southwest corner of the country the vital link continued, albeit with Rapides in new livery. Despite many attempts to produce a replacement aircraft through the years, there was nothing to surpass the type for operations from airfields such as St Just and St Mary's. Eventually BEA introduced Sikorsky S-61 helicopters on to the route moving the Cornwall terminal to a new heliport on the outskirts of Penzance. Most of the Rapides still in service joined Scillonia, a small airline

operating freight and passenger charters from St Just. Schedules were also operated between the airfield, Newquay and the Scillies in the mid-1960s. Re-equipment plans first centred around a pair of Islanders, but these were cancelled before delivery. Instead the airline began negotiations for two Twin Pioneers in Kuwait. In due course the aircraft returned to the UK but their new owner was detained, resulting in the demise of Scillonia. In the 1970s Land's End Aero Club maintained the airfield's links with the Rapide by offering scenic flights in G-AIYR, these coming to an end with the sale of the machine in 1978.

Apart from commercial and club flying, St Just has also been the birthplace of a number of replicas including a full-size Hawker Fury. The first Volmer Sportsman amphibian in the UK was also constructed on the site where many of the buildings date from the early days. In 1984 a new company known as Isles of Scilly Skybus began operations, but at first its ambition to offer fixed-wing services between Land's End and the Scillies was not approved by the CAA. Eventually the company received the necessary licence in 1987 so that operations could begin on 6 April. Using Islanders for the short crossing, in the three peak months of July, August and September, the frequency reached six sorties every day except Sunday. Thereafter, in the subsequent years the number rapidly grew until as many as 30 return trips were

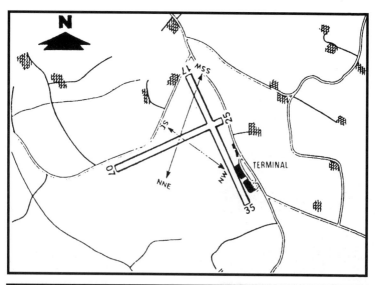

made daily. In 1994 the carrier reduced the size of the Islander fleet to three, but at the same time added a larger capacity Twin Otter for use on the longer sectors. Although it was acquired overseas, earlier in its career it had been one of Brymon's machines, so it was no stranger to the area. For many travellers the existence of an alternative mode of transport to the helicopter was welcome, so the service has continued to be well patronised.

Freight traffic still contributes a considerable amount of business for the company, which helps to compensate for the necessary reduction in the number of scheduled flights during the winter months.

Location and access: Situated 6 miles west of Penzance off A30 and west of B3306 from Crows-an-Wra. Ample car parking space charged at a daily rate. Short stays are free. A minibus service to and from Penzance BR station operates hourly for pre-booked passengers. A Cornwall Busways route to Land's End can be used, but this involves a 20min or so walk to the airfield from the nearest alighting point
Terminal: A part of the original prewar building, it has been converted to contain a lounge and buffet restaurant with sun terrace facing the airfield
Spectator facilities: None specifically provided, but all movements can be seen from the buffet

terrace. A 50mm lens can be used, but a 200mm is necessary for subjects parked on the grass in front of the terminal. There are also suitable vantage points for photography around the perimeter, the location being dependent upon the wind direction
Operators: Scheduled services by Isles of Scilly Skybus (Islander, Twin Otter). Various movements by the Land's End-based Aero Club and privately-owned aircraft. Westward Airways engineering facility handles maintenance and also the construction of replicas to order
Movements (1994): Figures not reported
Runways: 07/25 (2,221ft/677m), 12/30 (1,699ft/518m), 17/35 (2,598ft/792m) – all grass surface. Public transport flights use 07/25 and 17/35
Radio frequency: 130.7MHz (Tower and Approach)
Telephone: Penzance (01736) 788771
Operated by: Westward Airways (Land's End) Ltd

Below:
Land's End/St Just is the headquarters of the Isles of Scilly Skybus, the operator of the Islander G-SBUS. *A. S. Wright*

LEEDS/BRADFORD (YEADON)

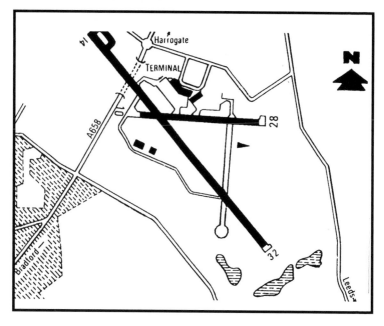

Although opened in October 1931, passenger services did not begin until an extension was completed in 1935. The Envoys of North Eastern Airways then connected the airport with Heston and Newcastle while West Coast Air Services introduced Blackpool and Isle of Man schedules.

Civil flying was suspended at the outbreak of war, September 1939 also seeing the departure of the resident No 609 Auxiliary Squadron to other bases. After becoming an RAF Station, Yeadon passed through the hands of several Groups before Training Command installed the Tiger Moths of 20 EFTS in March 1941. Early the following year this unit was disbanded and the airfield was transferred to the Ministry of Aircraft Production.

The nearby shadow factory was taken over by Avro, who subsequently built thousands of their products including Ansons, Lancasters, Lancastrians, Yorks and Lincolns. It was beneficial to Yeadon since it was necessary to provide runways, taxi-tracks and hangars to accommodate these aircraft.

After the war ownership passed to the MCA,

club flying being restarted by Lancashire Aircraft Corporation, who also reintroduced airline services. The Auxiliary Squadron returned, this time with Mosquitos, but the type gave way to Spitfires before No 609 finally departed in 1950. There was a lull in the activities at Yeadon after the MCA withdrew, but Yeadon Aviation assumed control after a time and flying recommenced.

Scheduled services were operated by BKS in the mid-fifties, serving Belfast, Düsseldorf, Isle of Wight, Jersey, Ostend and Southend, later adding Edinburgh, Glasgow and London. Another change in the airport administration came in 1959 when the Leeds and Bradford Airport Committee took over full responsibility. Soon afterwards other airlines began to use the airport, Aer Lingus introducing Friendships on a Dublin route, Starways using Viscounts on their Newquay service, while Silver City added Jersey and the Isle of Man to its network. Many of the destinations served by these earlier carriers are covered by the present day operators. In addition to the club, company and private aircraft based at Leeds/Bradford, the movements are increased appreciably by the activities of Northair Aviation, the Cessna agents for the area.

A new runway was added in 1965, while a modern terminal was completed in time for its opening in May 1968. A subsequent extension to runway 15/33 permitted the operation of larger jet aircraft although even this soon proved inadequate. After some ten years of discussions and inquiries, the decision to go ahead with a major expansion programme was taken in January 1981. Work began in 1982 to extend the main runway by 2,000ft/604m and the terminal area to give much improved passenger and freight facilities. When completed, it opened the way for transatlantic charters because such types as the 747 and TriStar could then be handled.

Undoubtedly Leeds/Bradford reaped the benefit of having its own locally-based commuter airline. Originally known as Brown Air when operations began in 1983, after adopting the title Capital Airlines in 1987 the company expanded rapidly until its constantly growing network was maintained by a six-strong fleet of SD3-60s and two BAe 146s. Introducing the latter type was a costly business and sadly it proved more than could be borne by the parent company, so Capital was forced to cease its operations at the end of June 1990. It was some time before a replacement carrier began scheduled operations, the newcomer being Yorkshire European. Several routes were flown by Bandeirantes, but towards the end of 1993 the company ceased flying. The operations were then taken over by Knight Air, which commenced flying to Aberdeen, Southampton and Belfast by the end of January 1994. Loads proved very satisfying and encouraged the carrier to upgrade its fleet at the end of 1995, replacing two of its three Bandeirantes with a pair of Jetstream 31s. However, before the latter entered service, Knight Air decided to cease the scheduled services to concentrate on its maintenance work. The carrier's routes were transferred to Manx.

Restricted opening hours have always been observed by Leeds/Bradford due to objections from the neighbouring residents. Consequently it has meant that some operators have been reluctant to base an aircraft at the airport because of the ban on night movements, although a modest concession in 1989 changed the closing time to 23.00.

Finally, 24hr opening was introduced following the successful outcome of a planning application submitted to the local authorities in 1993. It brought a massive increase in IT flights from the airport, with two aircraft from Monarch and Air Europa based at LBA in 1995 to cover the Thomson and Airtours programmes.

Location and access: Situated 6 miles from both Leeds and Bradford on A658. Car park charges graduated. West Yorkshire buses link the airport with Leeds, Bradford and Otley
Terminal: Contains restaurant, buffet, bar and lounge
Spectator facilities: There is an area on the first floor which overlooks the apron. This gives good views of all movements including those on the main runway. Fronted by tinted glass, photography is therefore less easy but none the less not impossible with care. Along the roof edge of a projecting canopy, the presence of a barrier creates an annoying obstruction and appears to serve no useful purpose. There are other vantage points to be found around the perimeter towards the ends of the main runway, while the hill on the south side of the airport reached via Bayton Lane also offers opportunities for photography. A footpath extending from the lane next to the golf course runs along the side of the runway and is well worth the walk for photographic purposes if not the exercise.
Operators: Scheduled services by Aer Lingus (Fokker 50), Air UK (Fokker 50), British Midland (BAe ATP, Fokker 70, Fokker 100), CityFlyer Express (ATR42), Gill Airways (Short SD3-60), Jersey European Airways (Friendship, Short SD3-60), Manx Airlines (Jetstream 31/41), SABENA/Delta Air Transport (Brasilia). *Charter and IT operators:* Air Europa (Boeing 737), Air Malta (Boeing 737), Airtours International (Airbus A320, Boeing 757), Air Transat (Boeing 757), Air 2000 (Airbus A320, Boeing 757), AviaReps/Air Atlanta Iceland (Boeing 737), Britannia Airways (Boeing 757/767), Monarch Airlines (Airbus A320), Onur Air (Airbus A320), Spanair (MD83). *Freight flights:* Emerald Airways (HS 748)
Movements (1994): Total 49,737 (air transport 23,002/positioning 1,269/test & training 2,016/club 16,620/private 6,275). Total passengers 815,468
Runways: 14/32 (7,400ft/2,250m), 10/28 (3,609ft/1,100m)
Radio frequencies: 120.3MHz (Tower)/123.75MHz (Approach)/121.05MHz (Radar)
Telephone: Leeds (0113) 250 9696
Operated by: Leeds/Bradford Airport Ltd

Top:
The windows in the buffet area at Liverpool overlook the apron.
A. S. Wright

Above:
For many years a member of Air UK's fleet, the Short SD3-60
G-DASI is now with Gill Airways and is seen taxying from
Liverpool's terminal. *A. S. Wright*

LIVERPOOL (SPEKE)

The planning stage began in 1928, with the first experimental passenger service two years later. Apart from a few token flights, transport movements did not increase significantly until 1933 when the airfield was granted an operating licence, although most of the activity was created by the local flying club. From 1934 the number of airlines using Speke gradually increased to include such operators as Railway Air Services, Midland and Scottish, Blackpool and West Coast Air Services, Hillman Airways, United Airways and in 1936 Aer Lingus with a Dublin route. As the traffic increased so the need for better passenger facilities became more urgent. A new terminal was completed in 1939 to cope with the fact that Liverpool had become one of the busiest airports in the UK.

Even before war broke out, Speke had been earmarked for military use, partly as a defence base for Liverpool, but particularly in view of its close proximity to the docks and industry. In 1936 No 611 Squadron moved in with Tutors and Harts, although by the outbreak of war these had been replaced by Battles. A number of fighter squadrons took up temporary residence to protect the city, but the production of Blenheims and Halifaxes by Rootes provided much of the military activity. In addition, the factory based at Speke assembled the incoming American-built aircraft after their sea crossing of the Atlantic. One distinct benefit derived was the provision of tarmac runways and additional buildings.

Unlike most other airports, Liverpool continued to handle a few civilian flights during the war, namely those to Eire and the Isle of Man operated by Aer Lingus and Railway Air Services.

Postwar domestic routes were taken over by BEA using at various times Avro XIXs, Junkers Ju52s, DC-3s and Rapides, while Aer Lingus continued its Irish service with DC-3s. Liverpool had also produced its own local carriers. For instance Steiner Airways existed with Consuls in the late forties, while Starways later successfully introduced internal scheduled services and ITs employing DC-3s, DC-4s and Viscounts.

Belatedly, control of the airport passed to Liverpool City Council in January 1961, whereupon development began in earnest. Runway 09/27 was constructed to meet modern requirements, backed up by new taxiways and access points. One of the existing runways was extended and a further apron area also provided to cater for the expected growth in traffic.

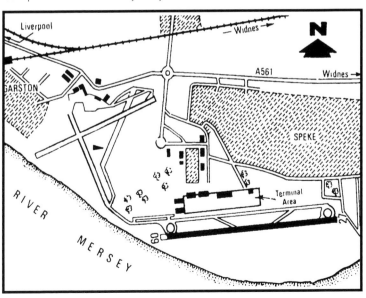

Cambrian Airways took over the Liverpool operations from BEA in the 1960s, continuing until the airline's total absorption into British Airways in 1972, after which the Cambrian name steadily disappeared. Services from Liverpool also declined, until at the end of October 1978 the routes were transferred to British Midland.

With the new operator timings were improved, although gradually the airline was obliged to adjust frequencies, destinations and equipment. Nevertheless, there was a greater determination to succeed than had been evident for some years.

In 1979 Liverpool was chosen as the centre of the Post Office mail flight organisation. After a trial period, the operation proved a great success and was soon well established with a building provided for the mail interchange.

The airport once again became the headquarters of an airline when Genair commenced operations in 1981. At first only the Gatwick route was flown, but in 1982 Amsterdam and Newquay were added to the network. Air Ecosse began scheduled services to Scotland, while Jersey European introduced Dublin and Stansted as their contribution, although both carriers soon closed down their Liverpool passenger operations. In November 1982 the Isle of Man services were taken over by Manx Airlines formed as a joint effort by Air UK and British Midland, an enterprise which has proved very successful and popular with all apart from the proprietors of the sea ferries.

The closure of the original airfield in mid-1982 concentrated all movements on to the single runway with the resultant lengthy distance to taxi to the terminal. Plans went ahead to provide a new complex; the control tower and apron being the first to be ready for use in the autumn of 1982 and 1983 respectively. Work started on the passenger building in February 1985, taking about one year to complete. Officially opened on 26 March 1986, a further month's work was still necessary before the new facilities could be used by the public. Therefore it was the 07.00 departure of the Manx SD3-60 G-ISLE on 28 April that marked the first movement outbound, the same company's aircraft G-RMSS having the distinction of becoming the first arrival 90min later.

Thereafter the volume of traffic remained very much the same, the only significant change coming in 1989 when Aer Lingus was forced to end its associations with Liverpool in favour of Ryanair. In the meantime it became known that the airport's owners were interested in selling a major shareholding. After carrying out project studies, British Aerospace duly acquired 76% of the share capital in June 1990, leaving the remainder with the five Merseyside local authorities. A new company was formed called British Aerospace (Liverpool Airport) (BALA) which quickly announced its intention to develop the site as the first major private-sector airport to be constructed in the world. In the event this ambitious undertaking took a leisurely course, with little sign of expansion evident by the mid-1990s. A public inquiry into the proposal to increase the airport's capacity to 12 million by the year 2030 was completed in 1995, proposals considered being an enlarged passenger terminal and the realignment of the runway. The latter would be undertaken to relieve the nearby residential areas of overflying aircraft, which seems an expensive solution to a common problem. General aviation companies were assured that access will continue to be unrestricted for the foreseeable future, a promise supported by the news that a dedicated building for such traffic was to be constructed. Towards the end of the year it was announced that a £10 million plan to improve the terminal and apron facilities had been awarded a grant of £4.7 million by the European Union. It coincided with the opening of a new road link between junction 6 of the M62 and the A562, resulting in a dual carriageway from the airport entrance not only to the south and the M56, but also to the north.

Location and access: Situated 6 miles southeast of the city off the A561. A pay and display system is in use in the car park. Trains run every 15min from Liverpool Central to Garston which is about 1.5 miles from the airport. Merseybus services provide the connection with the terminal every 30min
Terminal: Built in a modern style, the terminal contains a buffet and bar on the first floor overlooking the apron
Spectator facilities: None provided.
Nevertheless, the large windows in the buffet and waiting area ensure that all movements can be observed. Photographs can be obtained with care through the glass, provided a section can be found that has not been decorated by fingermarks and the like. Assuming a clear patch has been found, a zoom lens is preferable although the standard variety is sufficient for aircraft parked on the near stands. This vantage point is likely to become crowded at times,

making it difficult to secure a convenient spot by a window

Operators: Scheduled services by British Midland (Fokker 70), Manx Airlines (BAe ATP, Jetstream 41), Ryanair (Boeing 737). *Charter and IT operators:* Air Bristol (One-Eleven), Airtours International (Airbus A320), All Leisure (Airbus A320), Bond Helicopters (Dauphin, Sikorsky S-76, Super Puma), British Airways (BAe ATP), British Midland (Boeing 737), British World Airlines (One-Eleven), Brymon Airways (Dash Eight), Emerald Airways (HS 748), European Aviation Air Charter (One-Eleven), Futura (Boeing 737), Oasis (MD83), Pegasus (Boeing 737), Sabre Airways (Boeing 737), Spanair (MD83). *Freight flights:* Business Air (SAAB SF340), Channel Express (Electra, Herald), EI Air Exports (Short SD3-30), Emerald Airways (HS 748), Flightline (Bandeirante), Gill Airways (ATR42, Short SD3-60), Hunting Cargo (Electra), Jersey European Airways (Short SD3-60), Titan Airways (Short SD3-60), TNT (BAe 146)

Movements (1994): Total 80,223 (air transport 20,676/positioning 4,131/test & training 2,254/club 37,337/private 3,548). Total passengers 442,318

Runway: 09/27 (7,500ft/2,286m)

Radio frequencies: 118.1MHz (Tower)/119.85MHz (Approach)/118.45MHz (Radar)

Telephone: Liverpool (0151) 486 8877

Operated by: Liverpool Airport plc

LONDON CITY

For many years the idea of a city centre airport has appealed to operators but has largely remained a dream. A step nearer was taken in early 1981 when the Chairman of the Mowlem construction company discussed the feasibility of such a project with the Chief Executive of the London Dockland Development Corporation. It was the centre quay between the Royal Albert and King George V docks that was chosen as the site for such a scheme which would be only one part of the overall redevelopment plans for the derelict area. With the help of Brymon Airways, a trial landing was made by a Dash Seven, even then recognised as the type ideally suited to operations in the space available.

Planning applications were submitted, but in January 1983 it was announced that there would be a public inquiry which was not concluded until October. Even this did not allow much visible progress to be made and it was not until May 1985 that outline planning permission was given. During the waiting period much of the design work continued, so the company was in a position to submit the proposals for detailed consent at an early date, approval being received in February 1986. Nevertheless, it was still not possible to start the actual construction because discussions between the Development Corporation and the Port of London Authority lingered on, the obstacle being the ownership of the freehold.

Work eventually started in April, the first task being the demolition of the large warehouses and other buildings standing on the 40-hectare site. Progress was swift so that by Christmas the runway was completed and the terminal shell

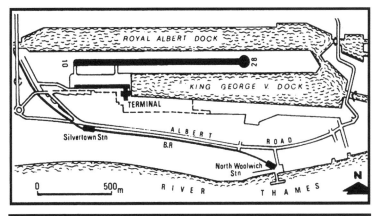

was roofed over. It was arranged that departing passengers used the first floor holding lounges at the gates before proceeding to the aircraft, seven stands being provided initially with space available for another three in the future. Facilities for those arriving are situated at ground level. As early as 1982, the CAA had to open a pending file as carriers began to lodge their licence applications. Brymon of course was the first in the queue, but was soon joined by such companies as Jersey European, Manx, City Air, British Air Ferries and Brown Air. After more serious thought all of these lost interest, leaving only Brymon and newcomer Eurocity Express as the contenders. Following the hearings the CAA approved both airlines' requests, so when commercial services began on 26 October 1987, they brought a duplication of effort in the Paris sector with Brussels exclusive to Eurocity.

After only a few weeks it became necessary to suspend the schedules to the French capital because of air traffic difficulties, but after a month flights were fully restored. In March 1988 a new name came into use at the airport when Eurocity took the title of London City Airways, at the same time announcing that a link with Amsterdam would be launched in May. There was then a long pause before a third company joined the pioneers at London City, but in September 1989 the Dutch carrier Flexair started operating schedules between the Docklands site and Rotterdam with a Dornier 228. Further international flavour was gained when two of Brymon's Dash Sevens were repainted in full Air France livery for use on new links to Strasbourg and Lille.

The airport's developers had realised from the beginning that in its present state the range of aircraft able to avail themselves of the facilities was strictly limited. It was therefore essential to extend the runway by 169m so that types such as the BAe 146, Fokker 50, ATR42 and SAAB 340 could be handled. Trials with the 146 were carried out in July 1988 and aroused very little adverse comment from the nearby residents, but it was not until 12 September 1989 that the necessary planning applications were submitted. This action motivated the Departments of Transport and the Environment to arrange for a public inquiry to be held during the summer of 1990.

Unfortunately, London City Airways was forced to contract its operation in the spring for economic reasons, with the result that Brymon took over the Amsterdam route. This move did not solve the situation so on 1 September, British Midland assumed responsibility for London City's remaining activities. At the same time the Paris route was dropped from the network leaving only the Brussels sector, albeit with increased frequency of service.

It was a sad end for the airline which had helped to establish the Docklands site during its first three years of existence. The decision came at a time just as the news was released that objections to the runway extension had been withdrawn. At least it gave fresh hope for the airport's future prospects, but was too late for the carrier.

Work progressed swiftly on the lengthening process, enabling the runway to become fully operational in the spring of 1992. It opened the way for a number of operators including Crossair, Conti-Flug and Malmo Aviation with BAe 146s, which then linked London City with Zürich, Berlin (Tempelhof) and Stockholm (Bromma). At the same time Air France ended its arrangement with Brymon and began operating its own services to Paris with Brit Air's ATR42s. Traffic has subsequently been steadily rising with various new carriers regularly adding new destinations to the airport's coverage. On the debit side, there have been several companies such as Flexair, Conti-Flug and Malmo Aviation which have been obliged to end their operations. Several types of corporate aircraft have received approval to operate into City, all such movements helping the facility to prosper. In late 1995 it was finally sold by Mowlem, with the new owner announcing that there are no plans to introduce drastic changes.

Location and access: The 6-mile journey from the City is via the Limehouse Link, a dual carriageway road which links directly with the airport. There are similar connections with the A406 North Circular plus the M11 and M25 motorways. From south of the Thames, access is either through the Rotherhithe or Blackwall Tunnels or the Dartford Crossing bridge. All routes are well signposted. There are both short- and long-term car parks available, the first hour in the latter being free. The Bank Underground station provides an interchange with the Docklands Light Railway which takes 12min for the journey to Canary Wharf. From the North Colonnade outside the station, the airport's Yellow Route shuttle bus completes the trip to the terminal in 8min, for which there is a flat fare. This rail service is only available on weekdays. As an alternative the Red Route shuttle bus links Liverpool Street Station with the airport every 20min on weekdays. At weekends the service is operated to coincide with flight times at a 30min frequency. A single fare is payable for the 25min journey. A bus service links the terminal with Stratford BR station (for Central Line and Docklands Light Railway) every 20min on Mondays to Saturdays and at 30min intervals on Sundays

Terminal: Contains landside cafeteria and restaurant at east end of first floor. Shops and bank on ground floor

Spectator facilities: None provided, but from the cafeteria a view of the runway is possible across the King George V dock. The ground level car park offers a better vantage point with photography possible ideally using a 200mm-300mm zoom lens.

Operators: Air Engiadina (Dornier Do328), Air France (Fokker 70), Air Jet (BAe 146), Augsburg Airways (Dash Eight), Business Air (BAe 146), CityJet (BAe 146), Crossair (RJ85, SAAB 2000), Denim Air (Fokker 50), SABENA (Dash Eight/RJ85), VLM (Fokker 50), World Airlines (BAe 146). *Charter and IT operators:* CityJet (BAe 146), Titan Airways (ATR42), World Airlines (BAe 146). Both Malev and Avianova were considering the launch of services in 1996.

Movements (1994): Total 17,341 (air transport 16,970/positioning 179/private 104). Total passengers 479,020

Runway: 10/28 (3,934ft/1,100m)

Radio frequencies: 118.4MHz (Tower)/132.7MHz (Approach)/128.025MHz (Radar)

Telephone: London (0171) 474 5555

Operated by: London City Airport Ltd.

LUTON

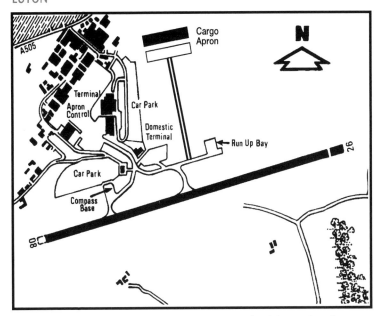

The grass airfield at Luton was officially opened on 16 July 1938. A need for larger premises had already prompted Edgar Percival to set up his expanding works at the new site in order to increase production of the Vega Gull. This type was developed into the Proctor, which began to appear in late 1939 to serve as RAF communications aircraft. During the war the company produced the type for radio operator training, while the civilianised MK 5 proved a success amongst the postwar small operators.

Percival's products continued to be adopted by the RAF. The Prentice, Prince variants, Provost and Jet Provost were all designed and in many cases built at Luton. By the mid-fifties the company was known as Hunting Percival, abbreviated to Hunting before becoming a part of the British Aircraft Corporation. The reorganisation brought aircraft production to an end at Luton.

The Napier engine company was also located on the airfield, while on the lighter side, the Luton Flying Club was re-established as soon as possible after the war. In the 1950s the airfield became the operating base for several charter airlines including Eagle Aviation's three Yorks, which were resident from April 1950 to November 1952. Scheduled services by Derby Aviation were available in 1959, the year that the council planners realised that their airport was beginning to fulfil its intended role. To help speed up the process the decision was taken to construct a new runway 5,423ft in length, a distance in due course extended to 7,078ft. It had the desired effect, encouraging both operators and passengers in such numbers that it soon highlighted the inadequacies of the old wooden terminal building. Consequently a brand-new £1 million complex was designed and built ready for its opening in 1966.

One of the newcomers to Luton was Autair, a helicopter operator which had decided to enter the air transport market in 1960 using an ex-BEA DC-3. By the time that the company started work in earnest the following year it had a fleet of three which were kept busy flying ITs. An entry into the scheduled scene was made in 1963 when on 1 October, Viking G-AHPL left the airport on its inaugural trip to Blackpool. Loads proved encouraging, so Autair purchased three Ambassadors to provide increased capacity, all entering service for the 1964 season. To develop its scheduled interests, the carrier acquired BEA's three surplus Heralds, taking over the BKS service from Teesside to London, later extended to Dundee. By 1969 Luton had seen a dramatic increase in the number of IT passengers handled and it was becoming obvious that Autair was clearly more involved in this type of work. As anticipated, all schedules were dropped from 31 October and from the beginning of the new year the airline became Court Line. Luton was firmly established as a holiday airport.

As more and more people poured through the terminal so it became increasingly inadequate. Then came the wide-bodied TriStars. In 1973 Court took delivery of two, each able to move 400 passengers, which did little to ease the overstretched ground services' problems. During the year a staggering 3,145,658 travellers squeezed through the airport, but it was to be the highest figure for many years. The collapse of Luton's busiest

carrier in 1974 reduced the total drastically to 1,920,275 in 1974/75. Although responsible for a major share of the airport's improving fortunes, Court was not alone by any means. Apart from Dan-Air's contribution, both Britannia and Monarch were playing a considerable part in the success story. Nevertheless, the collapse was a serious blow, but it did at least bring some respite and an opportunity for some terminal expansion.

It was to be 1978 before Luton became officially recognised by a Government White Paper as a fully-fledged international airport. As eventually a capacity of 5 million passengers per annum was envisaged, the Borough Council was sufficiently encouraged to embark on a major development starting in 1979 and taking five years to complete. Finally, when the new facilities were formally opened by the Prince of Wales on 11 July 1985, a far more spacious and modern terminal was ready for service. At this stage the capacity had risen to 3.5 million but the annual total number of passengers passing through was still under 2 million. There was therefore a need to encourage more airlines, especially those with schedules.

These have never been particularly numerous at Luton, for many years only a seasonal British Midland service to Jersey being available. An international route to Brussels was introduced by Euroflite in 1980, followed in February 1985 by a regular link with Amsterdam provided by newcomer London European. History was made in November when the first scheduled flight by an overseas company was made to Luton. Flown by Jetstreams of NetherLines, the service once again connected the airport with Amsterdam to augment those of LEA. Unfortunately, the latter's financial affairs led to the carrier suspending operations in February 1986 pending a reorganisation. Meanwhile the Irish airline, Ryanair, had been granted the licence to fly between Dublin and Luton, starting up in the spring with HS 748s. Such was the popularity of the route that One-Elevens were substituted and the frequencies increased until as many as seven return flights were operated on some days. As the company prospered so its network expanded, until by 1990 routes to Carrickfinn, Cork, Galway, Kerry County, Knock, Shannon, Sligo and Waterford had been added. In the process, 1988 had seen a start made to replace the 748s with ATR42s, while a pair of Airbus A320s were ordered for the early 1990s.

At the beginning of 1987 it was announced that the management of Ryanair had acquired LEA, its relaunch set for May. Brussels was the airline's main target for its single One-Eleven, with Amsterdam visited at reduced frequency. The latter service did not prove a success and was quickly withdrawn, but the Belgian link survived until the start of the 1989 summer season when it suffered a similar fate. Over capacity and timings unsuited to businessmen's requirements were chiefly to blame for the failures. It was therefore decided that LEA would use its solitary aircraft exclusively for charter work or substituting the parent company's aircraft. At the same time the operating name was changed to Ryanair Europe although its base remained at Luton. During 1990 the carrier acquired three of British Island's One-Elevens in order to take over the latter's IT commitments, particularly to Italian destinations.

In mid-1987 Ryanair gained a competitor on the Dublin sector when Virgin Atlantic was awarded the licence. At first a Viscount was leased from British Air Ferries, but in 1988 a pair of Club Air Boeing 727s flew the services for a time before reverting to the BAF machine. In the meantime Virgin had decided to concentrate on its long-haul activities, so Capital successfully applied for the schedule. Once again the Viscount was used initially, but it was a short-term expedient pending the delivery of the first of two BAe 146s in the summer. The Leeds-based airline went on to introduce other regular services into Luton, contributing an impressive amount of traffic to the airport. Sadly the carrier was forced to suspend all operations at the end of June 1990, which left quite a void in the airport's movements.

Ironically, in view of the growing number of domestic passengers, the authorities had decided to construct a separate terminal to help relieve the congestion in the main building. Due to open in early September 1990, only Britannia and Manx provided daily internal schedules at the time. In addition, British Midland ensured that there were seasonal links with the Channel Islands, while Monarch offered flights to Malaga, Malta, Menorca and Tenerife several times each week. In the late summer it was expected that Luton-based Air Exel would launch its proposed services with Brussels, Paris and Edinburgh, while in the Netherlands Freeway Air was due to take over the Maastricht run previously maintained by Virgin. In the event neither project materialised. A further reduction in scheduled traffic was suffered when Ryanair transferred some of its operations to Stansted in the spring of 1991, a loss offset to some extent by several Scandinavian carriers moving from the Essex airport to Luton.

Nevertheless, the airport was still not over-endowed with scheduled traffic. In an attempt to improve this situation, the airport authorities invited carriers to introduce new destinations with the incentive of a subsidy for a set period. CityFlyer was successful in its bid to provide a link with Paris (Charles de Gaulle) using an ATR42 for the thrice-weekdaily service after its start-up in 1994. The airline continued to fly the route until the end of the 1995 summer season, whereupon the service was taken over by Suckling Airways. This small carrier had been flying Waterford and Amsterdam schedules with its Dornier 228s for some time, but the latter type was considered too small for the busy new sector, so a Dornier 328 was acquired specifically for the route.

In the meantime another carrier had introduced a service to Belfast International to replace the lapsed Britannia operation. Emerald European was formed for the purpose and used a One-Eleven leased from European Air Charter for the flights launched in late 1994. Unfortunately, the airline was unable to maintain adequate frequencies and therefore suspended its activities in the spring of 1995 while the company was restructured. It reappeared as Emerald Air with a Boeing 737 leased from the French carrier, Air Toulouse, having ended its association with European Air Charter. However, the new operation failed to continue beyond the first sortie and the aircraft was returned to its owner.

After this set-back, Luton was chosen as the London terminus for the low-cost schedules proposed by a new carrier known as easyJet. This Greek-owned company launched its first thrice-daily link with Glasgow on 10 November 1995, being joined by an Edinburgh sector two weeks later on 24 November. The aircraft used for the latter flights had spare capacity during the middle of the day, so the airline was able to add an Aberdeen service to its network in January 1996. Following the success of the domestic project, the easyJet management launched an Amsterdam service in April, followed by sectors to Nice and Barcelona in June.

Executive aircraft make considerable use of the airport, often for attention by one of the resident engineering facilities. Mail and parcels traffic during the night is responsible for a large number of regular movements at Luton which is linked with various points around the UK and Europe.

Location and access: Situated southeast of Luton some 2 miles from M1 Junction 10. New direct link road to airport opened February 1996. BR's Luton Flyer runs at frequent intervals throughout the day with an hourly service between midnight and 06.00. It connects Luton with London King's Cross Thameslink with a journey time of about 45min which includes the coach link between the station and airport. Express coaches are available to most parts of the country, either direct or via London (Victoria), by using route 757. This runs every 30min for most of the day and hourly on Sunday taking about 75min for the trip. Services also operate to Heathrow and Gatwick. Local bus routes connect the town bus station with the airport, while there are express links with Peterborough, Northampton and Milton Keynes

Terminal: The main, northeast-facing international building contains restaurants, bar, buffets and shop

Spectator facilities: Car park and enclosure are combined alongside the taxiway. No admission charge but a daily flat rate for cars on a pay-and-display basis. Buffet available in adjacent terminal. Surrounded by a sturdy 10ft-high chainlink fence, the facilities are excellent for viewing all movements, but the barrier does make it more difficult to obtain photographs. A wide-angle lens is necessary for aircraft of Boeing 737 size. Mornings are best on sunny days

Operators: Scheduled services by British Midland (Fokker 70), Debonair (BAe 146), easyJet (Boeing 737), Manx Airlines (BAe ATP, BAe 146), Monarch Airlines (Airbus A320, Boeing 757), Ryanair (Boeing 737), Suckling Airways (Dornier Do228/Do328). *Charter and IT operators:* Air Malta (Boeing 737), Air 2000 (Airbus A320, Boeing 757), Britannia Airways (Boeing 757/767), British Midland (Boeing 737), British World Airlines (BAe 146, One-Eleven), Caledonian Airways (TriStar), Cyprus Airways (Airbus A310/320), Eurocypria (Airbus A320), European Aviation Air Charter (One-Eleven), Futura (Boeing 737), Leisure International (Airbus A320), Monarch Airlines (Airbus A300/320, Boeing 757), Sabre Airways (Boeing 737), Sunway (MD83), TEA Switzerland (Boeing 737). *Freight flights:* Air Foyle (An-124, Il-76), Atlantic Air Cargo (Electra), DHL (Boeing 727, Convair 580), Flightline (Bandeirante), Hunting Cargo (Electra), Southern Air Transport (Hercules), Willow Air (Bandeirante). Overhauls and repainting results in regular movements of aircraft visiting either the Britannia or Airline Engineering facilities. Similarly a wide range of executive machines are either based at or use Luton. The local flying club occupies the area to the east of the airport access road

Movements (1994): Total 41,588 (air transport 17,161/positioning 3,242/test & training 4,285/club 6,749/private 9,240). Total passengers 1,824,463

Runway: 08/26 (7,087ft/2,160m)

Radio frequencies: 132.55MHz (Tower)/129.55MHz, 128.75MHz (Approach)

Telephone: Luton (01582) 395000

Operated by: London Luton Airport Ltd

LYDD

Lydd Airport was built for Silver City in the remarkably short time of seven months to serve as the airline's UK terminal for its car ferry services. Given the appropriate name of Ferryfield, the airport's operational life began on 13 July 1954 with a Freighter flight to Le Touquet. Very soon Deauville and Ostend routes were added with the result that by the time of its first anniversary, over 34,000 vehicles and 88,000 passengers had passed through the airport.

The impressive figures continued to grow in the fifties and by the sixties other destinations had joined the routes radiating from Lydd, from where 100 flights per day were common in peak periods. However, very gradually competition from the new drive-on/drive-off sea ferries forced a reduction in frequencies, until by the end of 1970 all services had ceased.

Lydd was left without scheduled services apart from the occasional BAe (HS) 748 diverted from fogbound Ashford. The airport was also used for the storage of aircraft awaiting sale, but on 1 November 1974 airline movements were reinstated. Dan-Air's coach-air service was transferred from Ashford, resulting in the regular appearances of BAe (HS) 748s on the Paris route and seasonal Jersey operations. The cargo airline Air Freight also made the move with its DC-3 fleet, soon after adopting the title of Skyways Cargo Airline. It was not long before most of the previous inhabitants of Ashford followed suit, helping to swell the movements at Lydd considerably.

Dan-Air continued its coach-air service to Beauvais/Paris until the end of the 1970s, whereupon the long-established operation finally ended with the winter programme. Similarly the company ceased its summer only Jersey service in October 1979.

Hitherto, Skyways had for many years concentrated on cargo work. In the spring of 1980, the company took over the two Lydd passenger schedules using one of their two FH-227s. It was the first of its type to operate with a UK airline in this role, but proved very satisfactory, Unfortunately, in October 1980, the company ceased trading, its fleet being sold and dispersed. Lydd was entering another very quiet period, although Dan-Air was still using the airport at night for the purpose of carrying mail to and from Liverpool. This activity also ended in November 1981 when the airport was closed to all traffic.

For a time the future looked bleak, but fortunately the airfield was bought by Hards Travel who reopened it in April 1982. The company was an already established travel operator in the Birmingham area, but wanted to diversify its activities by offering ITs across the Channel using its own airline. Janus Airways was therefore formed, equipped with the ex-Brymon Herald in readiness for the inaugural run in December 1982. For the winter an average of four flights on each of five days were planned, followed during the summer by a much expanded timetable calling for some ten daily trips.

The airport's reopening was an event welcomed by those who had mourned its closure. During 1982 an application was successfully made by Instone Air Line to operate a Lydd-Beauvais-Rotterdam-Lydd freight route. A start was made in October, the aircraft used being a Bristol Freighter, the type which was responsible for the creation of Lydd in the 1950s. The airline leased a half of the existing hangar for in-line maintenance although its headquarters remained at Stansted. Janus Airways occupied the remaining engineering facilities.

In the early part of 1986 the airline was acquired by Euroair which carried on Hards' IT work unchanged. However, it was not long before the tour company was forced to cease trading which meant the end of the coach-air operations. For a time the future of Lydd was once again in jeopardy, but fortunately restricted facilities were continued for the benefit of the many transit light aircraft and local clubs. With new owners in 1987, the airport began to revive, although there were still no scheduled or IT flights. A good many improvements were introduced including a

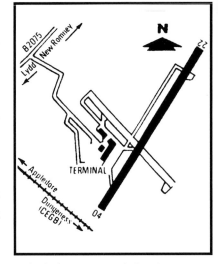

modernised passenger terminal and a new executive terminal offering conference facilities if required. A Category 1 instrument landing system was installed on the existing runway, while studies began into the feasibility of a second strip in the future. Lydd's new management began to seek airlines likely to be interested in providing regular services from the airport, particularly those willing to revive the London-Paris route. In 1988 Air Metro was well advanced with its plans to operate schedules from its Bournemouth base to a number of European cities including the French capital and Amsterdam. Each flight was to call at Lydd so it appeared that the latters prospects looked promising. Unfortunately, the CAA did not grant the necessary licences to the new carrier, which was found to be lacking the necessary financial backing. Ellan-Vannin Airlines then took over the troubled company expressing its intention to provide a similar network, but with Jetstreams instead of Metros. Meanwhile, at Lydd the check-in desks already optimistically displayed appropriate information for the expected passengers, which in the event never arrived because EVA also failed to start its promised services.

After these set-backs, hopes were raised again in 1989 when British Independent Airways applied for route licences applicable to the Kent airport. Although the airline was much in evidence during the summer, it did not begin scheduled operations until April 1990 with daily services to Le Touquet with a 748. A Paris link was commenced shortly afterwards using

Beauvais as the French terminal, although it was intended to move to Pontoise as soon as this airfield had received the necessary facilities for commercial work.

However, before this work was completed, BIA ended its commercial operations, leaving Lydd with only seasonal flights to the Channel Islands. Even these have not been operated regularly in recent times, the only commercial movements being those of Love Air which began to operate a scheduled service to Le Touquet. These flights were in connection with a short-break holiday programme, but eventually the operation was moved to Biggin Hill. Fortunately, the one-time ferry terminal remains a popular gateway for private aircraft heading to and from the Continent.

During the summer of 1990 Lydd was one of eight sites suggested for possible major expansion in the quest to satisfy the growth in air transport. Considerable redevelopment would be required before it could play its part and would involve lengthening the runway. One of the main handicaps in its present form is the poor access and ground communications. There has to be a distinct improvement in these if Lydd is to be seriously considered by travellers. However, like so many schemes of its type, it was subsequently filed with little likelihood of implementation.

Location and access: The lengthy airport access road is on the east side of the B2075 some 2 miles from its junction with the A259 near New Romney. East Kent bus services from Folkestone bus station take about 75min for the journey, but there is still a long walk to the terminal from the alighting point

Terminal: Single-storey building containing restaurant, bar and buffet

Spectator facilities: None provided. The large clean windows in the buffet look directly on to the apron giving an excellent view of activities. Photographs can also be taken through the glass although reflections are a hazard, with afternoons providing the best conditions on sunny days. It is also possible to acquire the occasional photograph through the fence adjacent to the hangar or along the access road

Operators: Scheduled services suspended *Charter and IT operators:* Varies year to year. Club and privately-owned aircraft contribute most of the movements

Movements (1994): Total 19,855 (air transport 46/positioning 260/test & training 822/club 11,098/private 5,641). Total passengers 212

Runway: 04/22(4,934ft/1,504m)

Radio frequency: 120.7MHz (Tower and Approach)

Telephone: Lydd (01797) 320401

Operated by: Lydd Airport Group Ltd

MANCHESTER (RINGWAY)

Ringway as it was originally known, was opened on 25 June 1938 to replace the inadequate airport at Barton. Domestic and international services were developed by Railway Air Services, Isle of Man Services and KLM. The airfield also had on site the presence of Fairey Aviation and Avro, both engaged in the assembly and test flying of aircraft for the RAF. Operationally Ringway was used only briefly by various units employed in the defence of Manchester, its main claim to fame during the war being its role as home of the Central Landing School formed in 1940. This unit was created to train paratroops, saboteurs and members of raiding parties from the lessons learned from the Germans in Europe.

The increasing use of the airfield resulted in hard runways being laid in 1941, followed soon after by a split in the responsibilities of the school. The glider element was posted to Sherburn in Yorkshire, while Ringway remained the base for the newly created No 1 Parachute Training School until March 1946.

It was June 1946 before commercial flying restarted, the first scheduled service being flown by Air France on the Paris route. Later that year Ringway became the home of No 613 Squadron which then remained until it disbanded in 1957. In the mid-1950s the need to expand the airport facilities was apparent, resulting in a massive programme of reconstruction starting in 1957. Five years later the new terminal building was officially opened which brought the airport up to a very high standard.

The advent of the wide-bodied airliners necessitated further development in the 1970s, when a new complex for international flights was provided plus additional car parks and approach roads. Manchester is now the largest UK airport outside London with services to most centres in Europe. It is also the terminal for North American, African, Middle and Far East scheduled services, while numerous passenger and cargo charters are operated by a variety of carriers, both UK and foreign. A shuttle service to London using One-Elevens and Tridents was started in the autumn of 1979 by British

Airways, these types later replaced by the Boeing 757.

Internal improvements to the terminal began in 1982, providing new style buffets, restaurant, coffee bar and expanded shopping area. Outside, rearrangements of the terminal access roads were designed to give additional parking spaces and a new bus/coach station. Enlargement of the western apron provided sufficient parking space for four Boeing 747s, while in February 1984 work began on the extension to the international Pier C. Other improvements continued to be implemented, but the next major change scheduled was the construction of a brand-new terminal exclusively for the use of domestic passengers. Costing £27 million, it was opened in the spring of 1989 to replace Pier A built in 1962. Although completely self-contained with its own restaurant, shops and multi-storey car park, there is a link way with the main concourse for the benefit of transfer passengers.

While the structure was intended to handle 2.5 million passengers annually, in the long-term even greater expansion was needed. In April 1988 approval was given for the provision of a brand-new terminal to be built for use in the mid-1990s. Situated to the northwest of the present complex, the site was already owned by the airport, although the diversion of a local road will be necessary. An interesting design was chosen with a two-storey building fronting the much-enlarged apron. The main concourse is flanked on either side by long fingers along which the various airbridge-equipped gates are positioned. Provision has been made for a remote island pier to be erected parallel to this structure at a later date, which will be reached by two underground passageways. Manchester International has now been given its own dedicated rail link with a station in the heart of the complex. When opened, the latest improvements to the airport were able to assist with the 14 million passengers using the facility annually, a figure forecast to rise to 20 million by the end of the decade. Plans are actively under way for the provision of a second runway, a scheme not accepted without objections from the local community.

Location and access: Situated 10 miles (16km) south of Manchester, directly connected to the M56 motorway at Junction 5. A large short-term car park adjoins Terminal 1 and is charged per half hour, rising swiftly after the first period. The long-term park is more economic for stays

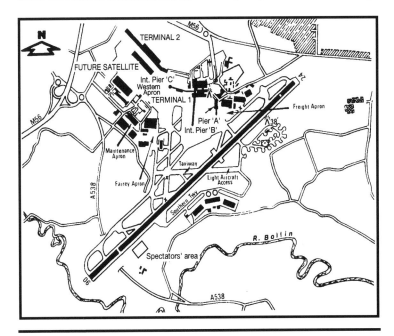

over 4 hours or so, while the Southside Saver offers both covered and outside parking at a cheaper rate. A direct rail service operates every 15min between Piccadilly/Oxford Road stations to Terminal 1 with a journey time of between 17min and 22min. Shuttle bus links with Terminal 2 are provided. Airbus service 200 runs from the city centre (Piccadilly) with a journey time of 25min. Other services link the two points but travel via different routes with varying journey times. Direct coach services are operated to a number of towns and cities in the north of England. Every two hours a National Express coach sets off for Heathrow and Gatwick, the latter destination reached in about 7hrs

Terminals: Now known as Terminal 1, the original building contains a restaurant, buffet and various shops. It also displays a large screen to commemorate the 60,000 paratroops trained at Ringway during World War 2. The adjoining domestic terminal contains a similar selection but on a smaller scale. Terminal 2 is also self-contained, although courtesy buses are used to convey passengers to and from the rail station, unlike Terminal 1, which has a covered travelator link

Spectator facilities: Through the years much of the roof terrace has been withdrawn from use as the terminal building has expanded. Now only the admission-free centre section remains available which is reached via an external stairway. From this vantage point most movements can be seen, but photographs are difficult to obtain without the aid of a zoom lens. Fortunately, the airport authority recognised the considerable interest shown by visitors and the need to replace the lost facilities. It was decided to develop the site of an old brickworks on the southwest side of the runway into a viewing area complete with car park. This was duly completed together with a mound for the convenience of photographers. The result has proved very popular with enthusiasts and casual visitors alike. Preferably, Runway 06 needs to be in use, when some excellent landing shots can be obtained, but even without this bonus the vantage point is well worth visiting. To find the area it is necessary to follow the airport perimeter with a series of right turns from the terminal, or off the A583 Wilmslow road

Operators: Scheduled services by Adria Airways (Airbus A320), Aer Lingus (BAe 146, Boeing 737), Aeroflot (Tu-154), Air Canada (Boeing 767), Air France (Boeing 737), Air India (Airbus A310), Air Littoral (Brasilia), Air Kilroe (Jetstream 31), Air Malta (Boeing 737), Air Sevchelles

(Boeing 767), Air UK (Fokker 100), British Airways (BAe ATP, Boeing 737/747/757/767), Cathay Pacific (Boeing 747), Continental Airlines (Boeing 757, DC-10), Crossair (SAAB 2000), CSA Czech Airlines (Boeing 737, Tu-134), Cyprus Airways (Airbus A310), Delta Air Lines (TriStar), El Al (Boeing 757/767), Emirates (Airbus A300/A310), Finnair (DC-9, MD80), Gill Airways (Short SD3-60), Iberia (Boeing 727, MD87), Jersey European Airways (BAe 146), Lauda Air (Canadair RJ), Lufthansa (Avro RJ, Boeing 737, Canadair RJ, Fokker 50), Luxair (Brasilia, Fokker 50), Manx Airlines (BAe ATP, Jetstream 41), Newair (Jetstream 31), Pakistan International (Boeing 747), Ryanair (Boeing 737), SABENA (Boeing 737), SAS (DC-9, MD80), Saudi (Tristar), Singapore Airlines (Boeing 747), Suckling Airways (Dornier Do228), Swissair (Airbus A320, MD80), Tarom (Tu-154), Ukraine International (Boeing 737), Uzbekistan Airways (Il-62). *Charter and IT operators:* Aer Lingus (BAe 146), Air Atlanta Iceland (Boeing 737), Air Club International (Airbus A310), Air Europa (Boeing 737/757), Air Ops (TriStar), Airtours International (Airbus A320, Boeing 757/767), Air Transat (Boeing 757), Air VIA (Tu-154B), Air 2000 (Airbus A320, Boeing 757), All Leisure (Airbus A320), American Trans Air (TriStar), Britannia Airways (Boeing 757/767), British World Airlines (BAe 146, One-Eleven), Caledonian Airways (Airbus A320, TriStar), Canada 3000 (Boeing 757), Centennial (MD80), CityFlyer Express (ATR42/72), Excalibur Airways (DC-10), Futura (Boeing 737), GB Airways (Boeing 737), Istanbul Airlines (Boeing 737), Laker Airways (DC-10), LatCharter (Yak-42), Oasis (MD83), Monarch Airlines (Airbus A300/A320, Boeing 757, DC-10), Onur Air (Airbus A300/A320/A321), Pegasus (Boeing 737), Rich International (TriStar), Royal Air Maroc (Boeing 737), Sabre Airways (Boeing 727/737), Spanair (Boeing 767, MD83), Sunway (MD83), Transwede (MD87), Viva Air (Boeing 737), World Airways (DC-10). *Cargo flights:* Air Hong Kong (Boeing 747), HeavyLift (Belfast)

Movements (1994): Total 169,908 (air transport 145,549/positioning 7,279/club 7,191/private 8,249). Total passengers 14,569,740

Runway: 06/24(10,000ft/3,048m)

Radio frequencies: 118.625MHz (Tower)/119.4MHz (Approach)/121.35MHz (Radar)

Telephone: Manchester (0161) 489 3000

Operated by: Manchester Airport plc

NEWCASTLE (WOOLSINGTON)

Passenger services began at the newly opened airport in 1935 when North Eastern Airways introduced routes to Edinburgh and London. Domestic routes were further developed up until the war, whereupon civil flying was suspended. Although requisitioned and used by the Air Ministry, Woolsington did not benefit from any development as in the majority of similar cases.

When commercial flying restarted, Newcastle did not regain its original routes immediately. In 1948 only a summer Isle of Man service was flown by Northern Air Charter, although the following year saw greater expansion with Lancashire Aircraft Corporation which set up a base at the airport. Operations had passed into the hands of Hunting by 1953, but before regular Dakota services could be flown, the airport had to be modernised. Several international routes were introduced bringing the airline's schedules in mid-1954 to 35 per week.

In response to this visible growth the airport authorities agreed to a programme of expansion to permit operation of the brand-new Viscounts then entering service. In 1955 the type was introduced on various Hunting routes out of Newcastle using the newly provided runway. However, despite these developments, passenger figures remained unimpressive, which resulted in the airline withdrawing after two and a half years of effort.

Other airlines continued to offer a few services, but BKS eventually became the major operator, restarting the London route in 1959. Subsequently the airline expanded its route network, eventually changing its name to Northeast to reflect its association with the region. Until its absorption into British Airways in 1976, the carrier played a big part in the development of air transport at Newcastle.

The airport has long been connected with one or other of the London airports. Nowadays British Airways supplies the Heathrow links, CityFlyer in the guise of BA Express flies on the Gatwick route, while Air UK offers Stansted as the southern terminal. In reality, in 1995 the sector was operated on the carrier's behalf by Newcastle-based Gill Airways due to a shortage of suitable equipment. The latter airline not only has a number of scheduled passenger services in its network, but is also involved in overnight freight work around the UK. Convenient connections for onward journeys into Europe are possible at Birmingham using the link provided by Maersk Air UK's Jetstream 31, a service pioneered by Birmingham European in 1989.

The expansion of the scheduled service network at Newcastle was in no small way due to the considerable development undertaken at the airport in 1966/67. At this time a new terminal complex was constructed in addition to runway and taxiway improvements. Further work was carried out on the terminal in 1981/2 which created more space for passenger reception, baggage handling, waiting areas, etc, while the pier modernisation programme

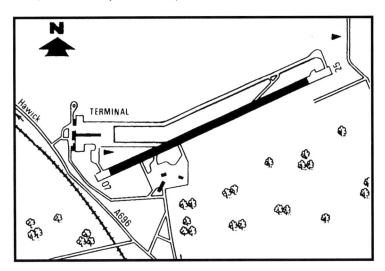

greatly improved the access to aircraft by passengers. Later in the 1980s the provision of a taxiway parallel to the runway removed any problems with congestion due to back-tracking. More terminal expansion became necessary in the 1990s in order to meet the demands of the traffic growth. Additional check-in desks were installed in 1992, mainly for the use of the IT passengers, the new positions taking the total in use to 36. On the apron two more remote parking spots for Boeing 757s were provided, which in turn made it necessary to acquire three more transfer buses. Work also started on a new £1.7 million fire station located to the north of the taxiway. The modern building possesses eight bays for the tenders, accommodation for the rescue crews and an observation tower.

Location and access: Situated 6 miles northwest of Newcastle on A696. Car park charges graduated. Central rail station is directly linked to the airport by bus service X77 which runs half-hourly with a journey time of 25min. Alternatively the Metro service from Newcastle Central rail station in the city centre to the airport runs every 10min with a journey time of 15min

Terminal: Three-storey building contains restaurant, bar, lounge areas, shop and buffet. Prices charged in the latter are expensive so it is worth while patronising the drinks vending machine located in the shop on the ground floor

Spectator facilities: A roof terrace open throughout the year gives an excellent view of all movements. Entrance is via internal stairs, admission free. A buffet is available in busy periods during the summer. Also an excellent vantage point for photographs, although a telephoto lens is necessary in most cases. Late mornings and afternoons are best in sunny conditions. The waiting area within the building is also a good observation point and is much warmer than the east-facing roof. Double glazing does not help photography

Operators: Scheduled services by Aer Lingus (Fokker 50), Air UK (BAe 146), Braathens (Boeing 737), British Airways (Airbus A320, Boeing 737/757), Brymon Airways (Dash Eight), CityFlyer Express (ATR42/72), Debonair (BAe 146), European Airways (Jetstream 31), Eurowings (ATR42/72), Gill Airways (ATR42/72, Short SD3-30/SD3-60), Maesrk Air UK (Jetstream 31), Manx Airlines (Jetstream 41), Sabena/Delta Air Transport (Dash Eight), SAS (Fokker 50). *Charter and IT operators:* Air Europa (Boeing 737), Air Malta (Boeing 737), Airtours International (Airbus A320, Boeing 757), Air Transat (TriStar), Airworld (Airbus A320), Air 2000 (Airbus A320), All Leisure (Airbus A320), Britannia Airways (Boeing 757/767), British Airways (BAe ATP), Caledonian Airways (Airbus A320), Futura (Boeing 737), Leisure International (Airbus A320), Sabre Airways (Boeing 727/737), Sunway (MD83), Transwede (MD87), Viva Air (Boeing 737). *Cargo flights:* Channel Express (Herald), BAC Express (Short SD3-60)

Movements (1994): Total 74,507 (air transport 37,153/positioning 2,687/test & training 2,119/club 16,462/private 10,400). Total passengers 2,458,969

Runway: 07/25 (7,651ft/2,332m)

Radio frequencies: 119.7MHz (Tower)/124.375MHz(Approach)/118.5MHz (Radar)

Telephone: Newcastle (0191) 286 0966

Operated by: Newcastle International Airport Ltd

NEWQUAY (ST MAWGAN)

Although built for the use of Coastal Command during the war, a small part of the site had been used for a time prewar by the first scheduled passenger services to Newquay. In 1947 the airfield was run down by the RAF, but for a few years seasonal civil operations were able to continue. A change of policy by 1951 found St Mawgan earmarked for development as the main Coastal Command base in the southwest, preventing any further airline traffic until 1959.

Services were then established to Liverpool and Glasgow by Starways, with routes to London and the Scillies added by Westpoint and Mayflower by 1963. About this time it was found necessary to provide improved terminal facilities, a small building being opened on 22 May 1965.

Newquay has seen a wide variety of aircraft types operated by a selection of carriers since the early days. At one point One-Elevens were used on the London service by British Eagle, but after the airline's demise in 1968, Dan-Air Dakotas and Ambassadors took over until British Midland became the licence holder. The company employed Viscounts and Heralds for this moderately patronised service, but the airline slowly built it up to give satisfactory returns.

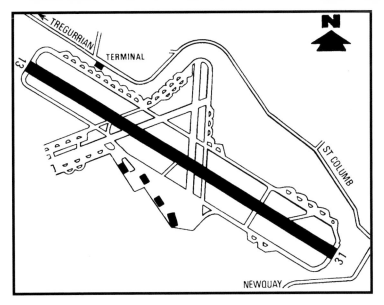

Rationalisation of routes found Brymon taking the route over in early 1977, at the same time assuming responsibility for the running of the airport facility. A Herald was acquired for use on the London service, although it was also employed on Aberdeen and Manchester schedules in between its normal duties or at weekends. This aircraft (G-ATIG) was replaced on the service in November 1982 when one of Brymon's new Dash Sevens took over the responsibility. The type steadily improved the loads carried until four return flights each weekday were justified, with a reduced frequency at weekends. In the mid-1980s the airline also introduced a seasonal link with the Isles of Scilly and Bristol which necessitated the use of a Twin Otter. By 1989 only one example of the type remained with the carrier, specifically for use on the sectors to St Mary's from Plymouth and Exeter. This kept the machine fully employed, so the direct Newquay run was dropped.

In the past other attempts have been made to provide the area with regular flights, but with little success. A new route was introduced in 1978 by Air Anglia, connecting St Mawgan with Swansea, Birmingham and Norwich. Like the Brymon service, it was aimed particularly at businessmen since no longer is Newquay purely a holiday only airport. However, the route did not prove to be an economic proposition and

was removed from the network after the 1979 season. In 1982 the Liverpool-based airline Genair introduced a weekend service from Merseyside using a Bandeirante. Loads were not exceptional and since the route did not play a major part in the company's future plans, it was soon dropped.

Apart from the scheduled movements, a number of executive aircraft are regular visitors.

Location and access: Situated 5 miles northeast of Newquay off B3276 and A3059. No charge for short-stay car parking. A Western National bus route from Newquay passes the terminal
Terminal: A more modern and spacious single-storey building has replaced the accommodation which had been in use since 1965. Recognising the need for expansion, a new structure was built as a joint project by Cornwall County Council and Restormel Borough Council in 1993. Sited near to its predecessor, it opened in March 1994 and contains a comfortable lounge area with hot and cold buffet
Spectator facilities: None provided. Viewing is possible from the area alongside the terminal or from the car park. Photography is possible but conditions become more difficult on sunny days, particularly in the afternoons
Operators: Scheduled services by Brymon Airways (Dash Eight), Isles of Scilly Skybus

(Islander, Twin Otter). Charters mainly by company executive types

Movements (1994): Figures not reported

Runway: 13/31(9,000ft/2,743m). It is a Master Diversion Aerodrome

Radio frequencies: 123.4MHz (Tower)/125.55MHz (Approach)

Telephone: St Mawgan (01637) 860551

Operated by: Brymon Airports Ltd (Civil). Ministry of Defence airfield

NORWICH (HORSHAM ST FAITH)

Horsham was built prewar but did not become fully operational until June 1940, although detachments of several squadrons were based here for short spells prior to this date. The Blenheim IV-equipped Nos 139 and 114 Squadrons were the first full time residents, but the latter's stay was of short duration. The airfield became the home of the first operational Mosquitos, No 105 Squadron taking the type on its inaugural mission on 31 May 1942.

Horsham was offered to the USAAF in late 1942, resulting in the arrival of the 319th Bomb Group with B-26 Marauders. By early 1943, P-47 Thunderbolts of the 56th Fighter Group had replaced the bombers, but soon moved on in order to permit work to commence on runway construction. On completion the airfield was suitable for heavy bomber use, thereafter becoming the base of the 458th Bomb Group which arrived in January 1944 equipped with B-24 Liberators. From the first on 24 February 1944 until the final raid on 25 April 1945, the Group flew 240 missions from Horsham,

dropping over 13,000 tons of bombs in the process.

After the Americans left in July 1945, the airfields reverted to RAF control. The Mosquito reappeared for a time, but the main type to use Horsham was the Meteor. The longest stay was by No 74 Squadron which remained for 13 years, 11 of them with this type. From 1956 until the end of the decade, Javelins of No 23 Squadron shared the base with Hunters, but by mid-1960 all the fighters had left. During the 1940s and 1950s the station was also regularly used by the auxiliary squadrons for their summer camps.

Plans to adapt the airfield into a civil airport for Norwich were well advanced in the early sixties, but it was not until 30 May 1970 that it was officially opened. Before this the runways had been fully renovated, landing aids installed and passenger handling facilities provided for the token services operated by Channel Airways. Norwich became the headquarters of Air Anglia, a newly formed airline which aimed to provide scheduled services for East Anglia.

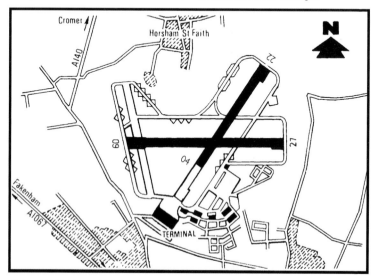

The routes and fleet gradually expanded until at the time of the formation of Air UK, the network took in Aberdeen, Amsterdam, Birmingham, Heathrow, Humberside, Jersey, Leeds, Newcastle, Stansted, Stavanger and Teesside non-stop. In addition, Bergen, Edinburgh, Glasgow, Newquay and Swansea were all served via one or two intermediate stops. This considerable traffic increase at Norwich had tended to outgrow the terminal facilities. In 1976/77 over 155,000 passengers used the airport, some 26% in excess of the recognised capacity of the building. By 1977/78 the figure had risen to 182,000, causing urgent consideration to be given to improving the existing facilities pending the provision of a new terminal, a project which could take ten years.

However, the pressure was relieved in 1980 by the steady cutbacks introduced by Air UK. By the summer of 1982, the network covered direct links with Amsterdam, Edinburgh, Jersey, Leeds and Teesside, with Aberdeen, Bergen and Stavanger reached after one or two stops. Frequencies too were much reduced with the exception of the Dutch services which have always been the most popular.

The licences previously held by Air UK involving Humberside and London were taken up by Eastern Airways. The Heathrow route was at first flown with a DC-3, which served a useful purpose in gaining publicity. Thereafter a Short SD3-30 was the standard equipment. The airline introduced an alternative London destination in 1982 when a Gatwick link was started. It was arranged to connect with the Humberside SD3-30, giving the Lincolnshire passengers the option of either London airport. The popularity of the service was such that an SD3-60 was substituted on some timings, a proportion of which bypassed Norwich.

In the autumn of 1982, Eastern merged with Genair and Casair to provide a more economic operation. The effect on Norwich was to increase the routes flown to include Birmingham, Liverpool and later Esbjerg, elevating the carrier to the position of the major operator at the airport. It was a situation destined to be short-lived. In June 1984 Genair ceased trading, leaving Air UK as the sole provider of scheduled services from the Norfolk airport, once again, the newly vacated routes becoming the target for several interested carriers. Successful in its application for the Humberside-Norwich-Heathrow link, Air UK was able to restore the sectors to its network after a couple of years or so with Genair. Otherwise the services on offer by the airline remained largely unchanged, although in 1987 a daily return

flight to Frankfurt was added, the Friendship staging via Stansted in both directions. Newcomer Holland Aero Lines introduced a route to Rotterdam in early 1985, but the Nomad-maintained operation was suspended at the end of the following year.

The engineering centre originally set up by Air Anglia continues to carry out maintenance and overhauls not only on Air UK aircraft but also on those belonging to other airlines around the world. All of this work had been carried out in the ex-RAF hangars which, although adequate for the turboprops, were not suitable for the new fleet additions. With the arrival of the 146s something larger was required, so a new jet base was financed by the airport authorities and built to the airline's specification. Occupation began in February 1990, the single-span building offering nearly 30,000sq ft of floor space and the ability to accommodate three 146s or two 737-400s side-by-side. Norwich is also used for the open storage of Heralds and Friendships awaiting new operators.

A new cargo centre was opened in August 1978 which offered greater opportunities for expansion into the freight market. Norwich was an early participant in the Post Office's nightly mail flights, the contracts regularly changing hands but usually calling for the use of Bandeirantes, Titans, Short SD3-30/3-60s or similar.

After many years in the pending file, the plans for a brand-new terminal were finally dusted off in 1987 for a start to be made on its construction. Originally expected to be located on the northern perimeter, problems in the planning stages dictated that it was positioned in the southwestern corner instead. At least this was nearer to the city and allowed direct access to the main road. Opened in 1988, the replacement building is a single-storey structure of modern design which could be mistaken at first glance for a low-level DIY warehouse. Nevertheless, it is practical and adequate for Norwich's needs. The airport later became one of the first in the UK to introduce security checks before check-in, a procedure due to become compulsory in the future. An extension to the building was carried out in 1995 for the benefit of KLM-ERA Helicopters' passengers. The latter company won a lucrative Shell UK contract to fly oil and gas workers to the North Sea rigs resulting in a boost to the passenger figures. The number of scheduled services increased in early 1994 when Interline introduced a Manchester link with a Jetstream 31. Rotterdam was added in 1995, with a twice-weekdaily service between the Dutch city and Manchester, but calling at

Norwich in both directions. In the event, poor loads on the latter route brought an end to the operation in November. By this time the Jetstream had been replaced by an SD3-30 pending delivery of an SD3-60. Plans were in hand for a Norwich-Gatwick schedule in March 1996, but the airline was forced to suspend its activities before the new venture was started.

Location and access: Situated 3 miles north of Norwich some 200m beyond the junction of the A140 Cromer Road and Fifers Lane. Car park charges graduated. An Eastern Counties City Line bus connects the airport terminal with the city centre at 20min intervals. The entrance in Fifers Lane still gives access to the Air UK engineering facility

Terminal: A modern single-storey building containing bar, buffet, shop and restaurant

Spectator facilities: A grass viewing area with picnic tables is provided at the western end of the terminal. Since this is alongside the taxiway it is a good vantage point for observing all movements. Unfortunately the 6ft fence is not photographer friendly, although the difficulties can be overcome. A 200mm lens is necessary for smaller subjects on the apron, but a 50mm is sufficient for taxiway shots although in this case it is not possible to focus the mesh out of the frame. Some extra height is therefore required to obtain a clear shot. Use of the tables for such a purpose is quite rightly discouraged, but alternative means of temporary elevation can be found

Operators: Scheduled services by Air UK (Fokker 50, Friendship), Suckling Airways (Dornier Do228). *Charter and IT operators:* Air Europa (Boeing 737), Air Malta (Boeing 737), Airtours International (Boeing 757), Britannia Airways (Boeing 757), Eurocypria (Airbus A320), Gill Airways (Short SD3-30), Leisure International (Airbus A320), Sabre Airways (Boeing 737), Spanair (MD83). *Cargo flights:* Business Air (SAAB SF340), Gill Airways (Short SD3-60) Numerous company and privately owned aircraft are to be seen, both visiting and resident. Air UK Engineering also handles the maintenance of a number of types, but particularly the Friendship

Movements (1994): Total 34,008 (air transport 8,128/positioning 2,278/test & training 18,275/private 4,387). Total passengers 215,835

Runways: 09/27 (6,043ft/1,842m), 04/22 (4,215ft/1,285m)

Radio frequencies: 124.25MHz (Tower)/119.35MHz (Approach)

Telephone: Norwich (01603) 411923

Operated by: Norwich Airport Ltd

PENZANCE

Penzance Heliport became the mainland terminal for BEA's Scilly Islands service on 1 September 1964. Earlier that year the fixed wing Rapides had been replaced by one of the new Sikorsky S-61Ns, although the helicopter continued to use Land's End (St Just) until the new heliport was completed.

It became the first fully equipped terminal of its kind in the UK, capable of handling passengers and freight plus having the facility for in-line maintenance work in a small hangar. The British Airways Helicopters operation was carried out with one S-61N, the aircraft being relieved by another of the type when major overhauls were due. After the sale of the airline this arrangement was continued by what is now known as British International Helicopters.

There was little apparent change in the operations with Saturdays continuing to be the busiest day for the services and Sunday still a day of rest due to the airport at St Mary's being closed. Obviously the holiday season provides a peak in the movements graph, with the S-61 shuttling backwards and forwards on its 50min return trip, the minimum time being spent in the turnaround. Since taking over, BIH has maintained the schedules with very few alterations, including the continuation of the sector to Tresco introduced by the previous operator in 1983. Objections were vigorously made against an application for a competitive route from Land's End/St Just, but on the second attempt Isles of Scilly Skybus were granted the licence for start-up in the spring of 1987. Fares were slightly below those of BIH, especially the popular day return. Despite all fears, the newcomer's presence had little detrimental effect upon the helicopter operation, with ample traffic supporting both modes of transport. In fact frequencies have subsequently been increased to both St Mary's and Tresco during the summer months.

Additional movements at Penzance have been generated by the need to support the rigs

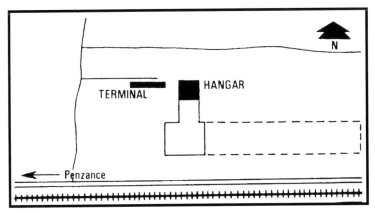

N

HANGAR

TERMINAL

Penzance

off the southwest coast, and the regular visits by the helicopters used by Trinity House to service the local lighthouses.

Location and access: Situated just under 1 mile east of Penzance alongside what was the A30 before the Penzance bypass was opened. Car park has graduated charges. A coach service connects the flights with the BR station, while a number of buses regularly pass the heliport to and from Penzance bus station

Terminal: The small building contains a bar, buffet and waiting area

Spectator facilities: Viewing is satisfactory from the terminal area or over the perimeter fence bordering the main road, although in the late 1980s the latter became a dual carriageway thereby reducing the width of the grass verge. Photographs from this vantage point are easy to

obtain using a 135mm lens, although the new fence is closely boarded and 6ft high.

Fortunately, it is not difficult to locate an object to provide the necessary additional height. At least if a shot is missed there is usually a second chance in under an hour. During the summer BIH operates scenic local flights

Operators: Scheduled services by British International Helicopters (Sikorsky S-61N). Regular visits by Trinity House (Bolkow Bo105) and others

Movements (1994) : Total 4,581 (air transport 4,210). Total passengers 88,855

Runway: Landing pad 100ft x100ft (30m x30m) with a grass manoeuvring area 09/27 (1,240ft/378m) parallel with the road

Radio Frequency: 118.1MHz

Telephone: Penzance (01736) 64296

Operated by: British International Helicopters

PLYMOUTH CITY

Originally a polo field, the site at Roborough hosted an air service as early as 1923 when a route linking the city with Birmingham, Manchester and Belfast was introduced. It was a little too ambitious for the period so the service was soon ended, the field returning to its more familiar role. At the end of the decade the same land was chosen once again for the use of flying machines, but this time it was to play the part of Plymouth's civic aerodrome. Arriving in the Westland Wessex demonstrator G-ABEG, the Prince of Wales officially opened the facility on 15 July 1931, although it was the local aero club that provided most of the activity until the Great Western Railway took a cautious interest in air services. Imperial Airways began operating between Cardiff, Torquay and Plymouth on

behalf of the company in the summer of 1933, later extending the route to Birmingham. As a result of this experiment Railway Air Services was formed, its first route linking Plymouth and Liverpool via Teignmouth, Cardiff and Birmingham. Great Western & Southern took over some of the operations in 1938, including the Plymouth network which by now covered the Scillies. A London flight was also offered, although this routed via the south coast airfields on its unhurried journey to the capital.

Used by the RAF occasionally before the war, in 1939 all civil flying was stopped and the airfield was requisitioned by the Admiralty. Communication flights were numerous, while target-towing aircraft worked with the Devonport gunnery school. During the summer of 1940 the Gladiator-equipped No 247 Squadron reformed at Roborough in readiness for the daytime defence of the city. A detachment was stationed at nearby St Eval for night operations. With Hurricanes replacing the elderly biplanes at the end of the year, the airfield was really not entirely suitable for the unit, so when the opportunity presented itself a move was made to Portreath. Target-towing and communications work then continued with a motley collection of types throughout the war until civil flying was resumed in 1946.

Subsequently Plymouth received the attentions of a number of airlines, all offering services to many of the traditional destinations such as the Scillies and Channel Islands. Dan-Air at one time operated a route to Newcastle via Bristol, Cardiff and Liverpool, but the Plymouth sector was later removed from the schedules. London has also been served both direct and via Exeter using a variety of types, but the physical dimensions of the airport always controlled the size of airliner employed and therefore the economics of the operations.

Since 1975 Plymouth has been operated by Brymon Airways, an airline which had started scheduled services three years earlier with an Islander. Its route network steadily expanded to take in Jersey, Guernsey, Cork, the Scillies, Newquay, Aberdeen, Gatwick, Heathrow and London City. Until Brymon took control, the small airfield was grass-covered, a description which gradually became more and more inaccurate under the scorching sun of 1975. It hastened the decision to lay 2,500ft of runway 06/24 with tarmac, followed five years later by a similar treatment for the second runway. Larger airliners could then be handled with greater

ease, provided of course that they were able to accept the length limitations.

Brymon used Twin Otters alongside the Islander from 1974, but in 1979 the last of the latter type left the fleet. In August 1981 the first of the company's Dash Sevens was received and early in the next year the type began to operate the daily Plymouth-Heathrow service. Later many of the Channel Islands timings were taken over by the larger machine, although the Gatwick and Scillies sectors remained a Twin Otter preserve for some years. Survival has never been easy for airlines in the southwest, so it was not surprising that in the early 1980s some reorganisation became necessary if there was to be a future. The new management succeeded in transforming the ailing company into a profitable airline by 1986, attracting the attentions of business travellers to the area by providing convenient flights to and from the capital.

Plymouth became a model for the new London City STOLport during the outline planning proceedings, each having a runway of similar dimensions. Brymon was involved in the new project from the beginning, using its experience at its home base to reinforce its claim to route licences when the time arrived. On 22 July 1987 the airline duly commissioned the world's first city centre, international airport, a status reached by the West Country site following extensive development at a cost of over £3 million. A runway of increased length and equipped with modern lighting and landing aids opened the way for a variety of new-generation regional airliners to serve Plymouth, now marketed as a Cityclass airport by the operator.

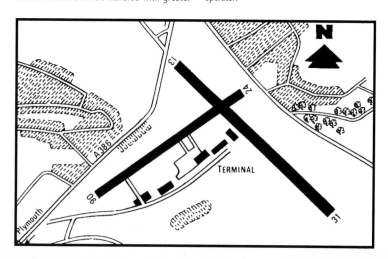

Brymon was merged with Birmingham European in 1992, the resulting airline taking the title of Brymon European. This arrangement ended in August 1993 when the pair reverted to their original status, although the aircraft were repainted in British Airways livery. Brymon became a wholly-owned subsidiary of the flag carrier, with its services marketed as BA flights.

Military aviation still flourished at the airfield, remaining the base of the Britannia Royal Naval College Air Experience Flight. This Airwork-operated unit was formed in early 1961 to provide some means of pilot selection for the FAA. Initially Tiger Moths were used, but in 1966 Chipmunks took over the duties, a type which remained in service for the next 25 years. The survivors were eventually replaced by civil-registered Grob G115D Herons operated by Short Bros on behalf of the Royal Navy.

Location and access: Situated 5 miles along Plymbridge Lane which is reached via Derriford Road from the A386, 4 miles north of Plymouth. Well signposted. Car park charges graduated. Plymouth Citybus, City Shuttle and Western National services pass the access road at regular intervals to and from the city centre
Terminal: An attractive single-storey building completed in 1982 contains a lounge area and hot and cold buffet, both of which overlook the apron. The accommodation was expanded in the early 1990s

Spectator facilities: None provided, but viewing is possible from within the terminal. Photographs can be obtained through the glass with care. The erection of new buildings alongside the terminal has filled gaps which originally offered vantage points, leaving only limited opportunities in the area. Good landing shots can be secured at the threshold of runway 24, although unfortunately the erection of a 10ft-high security fence introduced difficulties when attempting to photograph aircraft taxying prior to take-off
Operators: Scheduled services by Brymon Airways/British Airways (Dash Eight), Isles of Scilly Skybus (Islander, Twin Otter). Brymon's fleet is due to change in 1996 with more Dash Eights replacing the Dash Sevens, although the airline will retain a pair of the latter for work in Scotland. However, they will probably only be seen at Plymouth for maintenance purposes. Regular visits are made by executive types in addition to club and private aircraft
Movements (1994): Total 26,399 (air transport 5,453/positioning 498/club 10,286/private 2,596/military 7,202). Total passengers 94,253
Runways: 06/24 (2,467ft/752m), 13/31 (3,805ft/1,160m)
Radio frequencies: 122.6MHz (Tower)/133.55MHz (Approach)
Telephone: Plymouth (01752) 705151
Operated by: Plymouth City Airport Ltd

PRESTWICK

The mid-1930s saw many fields set aside for flying, one near the village of Monkton in Ayrshire opening in 1935. The Duke of Hamilton and the late Gp Capt Duncan McIntyre formed Scottish Aviation on the site, the company becoming responsible for the Tiger Moths of 12 EFTS and later the Ansons of 1 Air Observer Navigation School.

Known as an RAF station in 1939, it became a transit centre for many squadrons in addition to maintaining its training role. Scottish Aviation also steadily built up its repair and overhaul facility, but Prestwick's main claim to fame came with its use as the base for the North Atlantic ferry operations.

Thousands of American and Canadian-built aircraft staged through on delivery to the Allied forces, while 8th and 9th USAAF groups often made their first European landings at Prestwick. It was a remarkable station with a mixture of civilian and service personnel. Scottish Aviation retained much of the responsibility for the day-to-day organisation, controlling all catering, motor transport and works services. It was an obvious choice for a postwar airport.

It became second in importance to Heathrow immediately after the war, with various carriers including the airport in their schedules. Much rivalry has always existed between the Glasgow airports and Prestwick, but the latter remained the Scottish international terminal, probably assisted by its excellent weather record. It even became the headquarters for a new company in 1987 when Highland Express began operations with a single Boeing 747. The aircraft became a regular sight as it staged through the airport on its way to New York, or Stansted and Birmingham on the inbound sectors. Unfortunately its timekeeping suffered everytime the 747 displayed one of its frequent technical defects which did nothing to help the carrier's image. With costs escalating and still crippled by the expenses incurred at the launch, the airline was forced to cease trading at the end of the year.

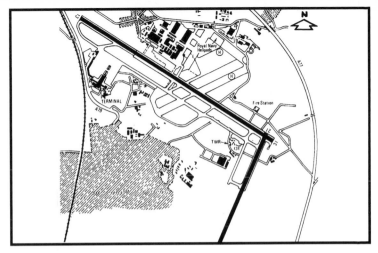

In the meantime Glasgow was preparing for a major expansion which would at last make it feasible for long-haul movements to be handled. Long before the new enlarged facilities were completed, pressure exerted by such as Air 2000 persuaded the authorities to allow the airline to operate its transatlantic charters from Glasgow in 1990. Not surprisingly, it was not long before the scheduled operators had followed suit which, of course, only added to the general congestion.

Passengers accustomed to Prestwick's spaciousness quickly noted the change because now there were domestic plus European scheduled and IT travellers in the terminal. Such traffic had always been very limited at the Ayrshire airport due to the undoubted convenient location of its neighbour. Not all the airlines transferred their activities, but there were sufficient to reduce Prestwick to a very quiet airport that hardly justified its continued existence.

At least there was an increase in the number of cargo flights, many being in connection with the overnight parcels and packages brought in by such as Federal Express and United Parcels. The airport proved ideal for this type of business which at the same time ensured that it remained active. After years without a regular scheduled service, there was a revival in 1995 when a link with Belfast was started by Gill Airways, while Ryanair commenced a Dublin run. The latter also set up a UK associate company in order to operate a domestic low-cost service between Prestwick and Stansted. A Boeing 737 was

transferred from the parent company for the purpose, but was intended to be replaced when the newcomer received its Operator's Certificate in early 1996. In the event, objections from other UK carriers resulted in the service being regarded as an extension of Ryanair's Prestwick-Dublin route, which meant that, as a foreign carrier, only 50% of the capacity could be used for the Stansted sector.

One of the long-standing reasons for Prestwick's lack of appeal was its distance from Glasgow and the time taken by the surface links. This factor has now been greatly improved with the provision of a BR station reached by a footbridge from the terminal. It gives the long-needed convenience of frequent fast trains to the city.

Apart from the commercial movements, the airport has seen Scottish Aviation produce Pioneers and Twin Pioneers in the fifties, followed later by Bulldogs and Jetstreams, both civil and military. By this time the company had become a part of British Aerospace, in due course taking the name Jetstream Aircraft with the responsibility for the production of the new Jetstream 41, the restyled ATP known as the Jetstream 61 and major sections of the Avro RJ series. Prior to this development, BAe had opened a flying training college equipped with a fleet of Warriors and Senecas, the location being ideal from the weather and traffic point of view.

Much overhaul and repair work has been carried out for military forces, particularly the RCAF and later CAF. In the postwar years Scottish Aviation had also operated its own airline on both scheduled and charter work, but commercial flying ended in November 1960, mainly as a result of the termination of trooping contracts.

For many years the USAF maintained its own base at Prestwick, not only handling the numerous transit flights, but also its air-sea rescue unit. After closing down the American facility, the site became HMS *Gannet* on 23 November 1971 for the use of No 819 Squadron's Sea Kings.

Location and access: Situated some 30 miles south of Glasgow via the A77 to a point about 7 miles south of Kilmarnock. The A78 and A79 lead to the airport. The route is well signposted from central Glasgow. The car parks have graduated charges. Buses connect with scheduled flight arrivals and departures by running between the airport and Buchanan Street bus station in the city centre. A similar service operates to Edinburgh (St Andrew's bus station). A more frequent bus service runs half-hourly between Glasgow (Anderson Cross and Buchanan Street) and Ayr which routes via the airport. There is a frequent train service from Glasgow (Central) to Prestwick Airport station which is linked with the terminal by a direct walkway
Terminal: Contains buffet, bar, restaurant, shop and spacious lounge areas
Spectator facilities: A terrace is provided on the second floor overlooking the apron and runway. There is no charge for admission. Excellent views are afforded of all movements, while it is also possible to obtain good photographs, although this is normally with the assistance of a telephoto lens. Lighting conditions are favourable for most of the day when sunny. Alternative spots can be found around the perimeter which provide different backgrounds and angles for photographs
Operators: Scheduled services by Gill Airways (ATR72, Short SD3-60), Ryanair UK (Boeing 737). *Charter and IT operators:* American Trans Air (TriStar), Air Transat (Boeing 757, TriStar), Air 2000 (Airbus A320), Brymon Airways (Dash Eight), Caledonian Airways (Airbus A320), Futura (Boeing 737), Oasis (MD83), Transavia (Boeing 737). *Cargo flights:* Cargolux (Boeing 747), Federal Express (DC-10, MD11), Lufthansa (Boeing 747), Polar Air Cargo (Boeing 747), Southern Air Transport (Boeing 747)
Movements (1994): Total 68,186 (air transport 2,436/test & training 22,494/club 24,449/private 10,164/military 5,889). Total passengers 137,787
Runways: 13/31 (9,800ft/2,987m), 03/21 (6,000ft/1,829m)
Radio frequencies: 118.15MHz (Tower)/120.55MHz (Approach)
Telephone: Prestwick (01292) 479822
Operated by: PIK Ltd

SCILLY ISLES (ST MARY'S)

Although the Scilly Isles were linked to Land's End by scheduled service from 1937, it was 1940 before the present airfield was opened allowing the RAF to station a detachment of No 87 Squadron at St Mary's. Operations from the field proved very successful, Luftwaffe flying boats frequently falling victim to the squadron's Hurricanes. The civilian service to the mainland was flown throughout the war at frequencies far in excess of the prewar schedules due to the

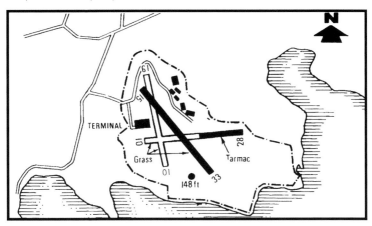

heavy demands of the military occupants. One aircraft was lost during the war, believed shot down by a patrolling Ju88.

After the war the route was maintained by BEA's Rapides, joined by several independent airlines through the years. In 1964 the fixed wing aircraft on the Land's End sector was replaced by Sikorsky S-61N helicopters, the mainland terminal moving soon afterwards to a new heliport in Penzance.

For many years the Scillies were also connected to Exeter, Bristol and Plymouth by the Twin Otters of Brymon Airways, which gave the opportunity for onward flights to London, the Midlands, Holland and France. These benefits were lost in 1990 when the service was withdrawn. An additional link with the mainland was provided by Isles of Scilly Skybus in 1987 when it began services to Land's End/St Just using Islanders. The company later restored the route from Exeter, Plymouth, Newquay and Bristol.

Despite its small size and its notorious hump-backed surface, the airfield handles a surprisingly large number of visiting light aircraft especially in the summer months. For many years any form of development was opposed, but in 1990 agreement was reached on the proposal to create a hard runway and at the same time add a modest extension to its length. Whether this will attract a new carrier remains to be seen.

Since 1983, the adjacent island of Tresco has been visited several times each day during the summer season by scheduled helicopter services from Penzance. A heliport with a 30m-square grass landing pad is provided about ³/₄-mile north of the southern edge of the island and is operated by Tresco estates.

Location and access: Situated 1 mile east of Hugh Town on St Mary's island. A bus connects with all BIH flights, while a minibus is provided for the benefit of Skybus passengers
Terminal: Contains waiting area, buffet and bar
Spectator facilities: Vicinity of terminal
Operators: Scheduled services by British International Helicopters (Sikorsky S-61N), Isles of Scilly Skybus (Islander, Twin Otter). Public transport is normally limited to operations by Islanders, Twin Otters or Short Skyvan Srs 3. Brymon took a Dash Seven to the island after the runway work had been completed, but the type was never used for regular services
Movements (1994): 11,425 (air transport 10,304/private 837). Total passengers 110,011
Runways: 01/19 (1,378ft/420m – grass – helicopter runway), 10/28 (1,716ft/523m — grass and tarmac), 15/33 (1,968ft/600m)
Radio frequency: 123.15MHz (Tower and Approach)
Telephone: Scillonia (01720) 422677
Operated by: Council of the Isles of Scilly

SHEFFIELD

Despite the enthusiastic launch of the project in 1988, the new airport for Sheffield has yet to materialise. The original plan to continue with the excavation of the coal on the site was carried out, at which point in 1992 the developers were due to commence the construction work. Unfortunately, the company assigned to the task ceased trading, leaving Sheffield Corporation with the problem of finding a replacement. This was not achieved until the beginning of 1996, when it was announced that the project was being revived, with operations from the new airport planned to start at the end of 1997.

SHOREHAM

Flying was introduced at Shoreham prior to World War 1, during which various RFC squadrons were based here. During the 1920s the Miles brothers were actively engaged in aircraft repair and overhaul, but it was 1934 before the airfields possessed any passenger services. Portsmouth, Southsea and Isle of Wight Aviation began by linking Shoreham with Portsmouth and Bournemouth, a route which continued to be flown until the war.

During 1939, Shoreham became the home of 16 E&RFTS, but at the outbreak of war it came into the Kenley sector as an advanced base. Numerous squadrons paid brief visits, particularly for gunnery practice in conjunction with the resident target-towing Lysanders. The same type was also employed for air-sea rescue duties from the airfield. The period around D-Day saw the Spitfires of No 345 Squadron busy on operations over France, but by August

1944 the unit had moved on, the remaining occupants following suit by the end of the year.

In March 1946 the airfield was handed to the MCA, whereupon civil flying recommenced. Scheduled operations were restarted in 1948 by Brooklands Aviation using Rapides on a Shoreham-Cowes-Southampton service. The company added Jersey to their route network the following year, flown via Southampton, but at the end of the 1950 season Brooklands withdrew from the commercial scene. Other carriers were also given route approvals including Air Enterprises and Island Air Services. Eventually the last named became the only airline to include Shoreham in its network, continuing until the end of 1962 when services were withdrawn.

JF Airlines introduced a new Jersey service in the early seventies, but lack of Customs at Shoreham meant that the inbound flights routed via Portsmouth. After a short break in operations, services were recommenced in the spring of 1973 to Jersey and Guernsey using an Islander and Trislander. Although successful, the airline was forced to terminate its activities with the closure of Portsmouth airport at the end of that year. Intra later acquired the licences, although the routes were flown by Haywards Aviation using an Aztec or Islander. In 1979 the company introduced a Dieppe route, while Aurigny Air Services added an Alderney to Shoreham link to its network. Neither of these carriers continued for very long on their respective sectors, although the latter was served for a time by Jersey European. The company was already flying the Jersey schedules

with Twin Otters, but rationalisation in the mid-1980s found the Islanders of South East Air operating this route on the licence holder's behalf in 1986.

Prior to the following season the airline was given authority to maintain the route in its own right which resulted in the equipment being upgraded to a Twin Otter. Unfortunately this development was short-lived since the carrier was forced to cease trading in early 1988. This time there were no operators interested in taking over the Channel Islands schedules from Shoreham, so the airport lost its limited commercial services. Nevertheless, the small check-in area still displayed South East Air's advertising in the summer of 1990 while awaiting some new enterprise to resume flights. At the beginning of the year there had been hopeful signs because Lydd-based Channel Air Shuttle submitted an application to the CAA for approval to fly on routes to Caen and Le Touquet.

One of the airfield's major disadvantages so far as airline movements were concerned was the lack of a hard runway. This was rectified in the early 1980s by the provision of 03/21 alongside the existing grass strip. Ironically all of the services operating into Shoreham in recent years have used equipment with STOL capability, but for the future it may well be a deciding factor for airlines in doubt.

A good deal of private, club, school and executive flying takes place, added to by the activities of resident air-taxi, sales and engineering companies. Shoreham is also the HQ of the Popular Flying Association.

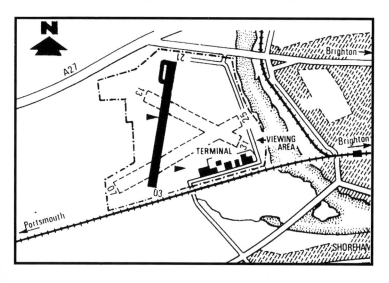

Location and access: Situated 1 mile west of Shoreham-by-Sea and reached from A27 or A259. Both accesses are signposted, but that via the latter passes under a bridge with 7ft headroom. Car park free. The bus service running between Brighton (Pool Valley) and Worthing passes the access road but involves a lengthy walk from the nearest stop. Journey time is about 30min

Terminal: Contains restaurant, buffet, bar and lounge area

Spectator facilities: Enclosure in front of terminal gives excellent views of movements and parked aircraft. A viewing area is also provided on the grass at the eastern perimeter. Both vantage points give good photographic opportunities, particularly when the wind is from a westerly point

Operators: Scheduled services suspended

Movements (1994): Total 63,664(air transport 1,425/club 36,778/private 20,372. Total passengers 2,774

Runways: 03/21(2,703ft/824m), 07/25 (2,982ft/909m – grass), 13/31 (1,394ft/425m – grass)

Radio frequencies: 125.4MHz (Tower)/123.15MHz (Approach)

Telephone: Shoreham-by-Sea (01273) 452304

Operated by: Brighton, Hove and Worthing

SOUTHAMPTON (EASTLEIGH)

Although it was 1947 before the site was chosen by the military for development into an aircraft depot, some brief aerial excursions had been made from Eastleigh during 1910/11. With the construction of four hangars and other buildings well under way, the airfield was transferred to American control in April 1918 for use as an assembly point for equipment arriving from the US. Its active life as a Naval Air Base was short, the armistice in November almost immediately bringing a halt to any expansion. By April 1919 the Americans had gone, leaving Eastleigh to revert to RAF ownership. For a time the base was used for storage purposes, but finally it was closed in May 1920 to become the Atlantic Park Hostel, a centre for housing European immigrants awaiting transport to America.

Towards the end of the decade municipal airports were becoming popular, so it was not surprising that Southampton's civic authorities began to explore the possibilities for the city.

Such sites as Fawley Marshes at Calshot and Chilworth were considered, but it was Atlantic Park which was chosen. Although purchased in 1929, it was November 1932 before Eastleigh was officially opened as an airport. Meanwhile, in the previous August, one of Sir Alan Cobham's famous air displays was held, a highlight being the arrival of Jim Mollison in his Puss Moth G-ABXY. He had used this machine when he became the first person to fly solo across the Atlantic from east to west.

A scheduled service using Airspeed Couriers was started in 1934 between Southampton and Hull, a link with Portsmouth was maintained and Railway Air Services began a mail run. With Jersey Airways moving its activities from Portsmouth in 1935, the increase in services operated was considerable. It was not long before Southampton was elevated to the ranks of the 'big four' – the others being Croydon, Heston and Liverpool. Air mail flights were

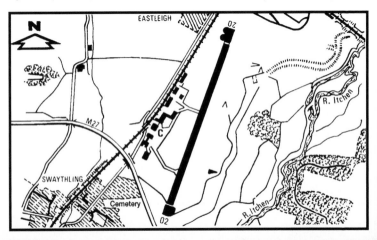

introduced to the Channel Islands with the opening of the new airport at Jersey in March 1937, the inaugural sorties being in the hands of Rapide G-ADBW and DH86 G-ACYF. Impressive traffic figures were achieved with 25,266 passengers using the schedules from Southampton during the year in addition to the uplift of 700,000lb of freight and 135,000lb of mail.

Even in those days the airport enjoyed good rail and road access which accounts for its popularity. For the next couple of years or so the schedules were in the hands of Guernsey and Jersey Airways which flew to both of the main Channel Islands; Great Western and Southern Airlines with its links with Brighton and Bristol; while Portsmouth, Southsea and Isle of Wight Aviation concentrated on providing a shuttle between Southampton and Ryde, IoW. The latter was a 10min flight and was well patronised as an alternative to the sea crossing of over one hour. In 1939 the single air fare was 7s 9d (39p) with a period return set at 15s - (75p) although a day excursion was available at 1s - (5p) less.

A certain amount of traffic was lost as a result of competition from Portsmouth, Shoreham and Exeter, but plans were soon made to counter this threat. Larger airliners such as the new Flamingo were coming into service, so the authorities decided to construct a modern terminal building at an estimated cost of £50,000. Completion was expected by the end of 1939 and it was to contain full restaurant and hotel facilities. It was confidently anticipated that services to the Continent would commence fairly quickly, especially since KLM had already operated a proving flight to Amsterdam and Swissair staff had inspected the airport. Understandably, however, work on the new project was shelved in view of the deteriorating European situation, but strangely it took another 50 years or so before a start on a new complex was contemplated.

Of course, the prewar operations had not been confined to civil flying with both the RAF and FAA making considerable use of the facilities. In fact the Admiralty assumed responsibility for the airfield on 1 July 1939 whereupon it was given the identity of HMS *Raven*. This nautical flavour then remained with Eastleigh until May 1946, although in the meantime scheduled air services with the Channel Islands had been resumed.

Commercial flying therefore played an important role in the life of the airport in the 1930s, but there was a significant event on 5 March 1936 that was to leave its mark on

history. On this day the Spitfire was first flown after being designed and built locally.

Another company to take up residence for the production of its own aircraft was Cunliffe-Owen, although it spent much of the war modifying or assembling machines of other manufacturers. Later the twin-engined Concordia airliner was conceived, the machine first flying on 19 May 1947. Sadly there was little hope for large-scale sales due to the prevailing economic situation worldwide, so production was abandoned. It also marked the end of Cunliffe-Owen's involvement in aviation, the factory becoming the property of the Ford Motor Company.

Always associated with rotary-wing designs, the Cierva Company was also installed at Eastleigh in a bid to produce its own helicopter. This was achieved, but the technique was still in its infancy and was proving expensive. After some success with the enormous Air Horse, the loss of the prototype hastened the end of an original design. Saunders-Roe took over the Eastleigh plant, remaining until it too was the subject of a take-over in 1959.

Air services began again in September 1945 when the Jersey route was reinstated, gradually increasing until by 1949 Southampton was once again amongst the busiest airports in the UK. However, without some expansion and a general improvement in the facilities on offer to both airlines and public, this position could not be maintained. Unfortunately, there were no signs of any interest in the suspended 1939 project, so as an interim measure one of the original hangars was pressed into service for passenger handling. This worthy if somewhat unsuitable structure continued in this guise into the 1990s, albeit with regular improvements to its spartan interior as the years passed. Nevertheless, the premises did little to revive Southampton's flagging fortunes in the immediate postwar period.

In 1952 Silver City introduced some new life by commencing a car ferry service to Cherbourg on 10 January, for which purpose two Bristol Freighters were based at the south coast airport. The carrier also proposed in 1953 to inaugurate a similar operation to Bembridge, IoW, but in the event it was not possible at the time due to bad weather delaying improvements to the island's grass airfield. Subsequently car ferry services were flown from Southampton to Jersey, Guernsey, Le Havre and Deauville with highly satisfactory results, but gradually the competition from modern ships brought an end to this enterprise.

In the meantime, on 15 June 1954, the

airport became the southern terminal for the first passenger service by a British-designed and built helicopter. This notable event was marked by the introduction of a link with London, the initial sortie being flown by the Bristol 171 G-AMWH which took 50min to complete the journey. Thereafter there was a return flight every weekday, but although load factors averaged 85%, it was hardly a profitable exercise, so after one year the route was suspended.

Surprisingly Southampton still had no hard runways in the late 1950s, which caused considerable problems for the heavy Freighters during wet weather. In desperation the operators were therefore obliged to move their operations to Bournemouth as a temporary measure. It could reasonably have been expected that this would have sparked a degree of interest within the Ministry of Aviation, which still controlled the fortunes of the airport. Presumably the news prompted an inspection of the case because it was duly announced in 1961 that it had been decided that Southampton was no longer an economic proposition and would be closed. Fortunately, the City Corporation thought otherwise and quickly took over the airport, leasing it to Southampton Airport Ltd for operational purposes. It speeded the decision to provide a runway, the formal opening on 25 September 1965 bringing an almost immediate return of airlines from Hurn.

The destinations served changed very little for some years, the Channel Islands accounting for the majority of the schedules. As the 1980s began, so there came a marked reduction in the number of routes flown from Southampton , until in the summer of 1982 apart from Jersey and Guernsey, Air UK connected the airport only with Amsterdam, while Aurigny served Alderney. A far cry from the days of Paris, Dublin, Belfast, Brussels *et al*. Slowly matters began to improve, especially when the Dutch carrier Nether Lines took over the Amsterdam schedules with improved frequencies in 1986. Even British Airways returned after an absence of some years, introducing an Aberdeen-Edinburgh-Birmingham-Southampton weekday return trip with HS 748s, but probably the biggest impact came when British Air Ferries and its subsidiary Guernsey Airlines joined Air UK on the busy sectors to the Channel Islands. Using SD3-30s, SD3-60s and Viscounts, the companies attracted a considerable amount of traffic with fares set at a reasonable level. Together the airlines gave Southampton a new lease of life, re-establishing it as a major gateway from Jersey and Guernsey.

During the summer the news was released that BAF intended to sell Guernsey Airlines to Aurigny Air Services, but it was expected that operations would continue unchanged using aircraft leased from the previous owner. It therefore came as a great blow to the airport when it was learned that the airline intended to drop Southampton completely from its schedules with effect from October. Efforts were intensified to find a new operator to restore the highly popular services, one company which submitted a licence application to the CAA being Atlantic Air Transport.

Trading as Air Atlantique, the airline was normally associated with DC-3s and cargo work, so the entry into the turbulent world of scheduled services was a new experience for the company. Certainly its approach to the operation was novel because it announced its intention to sell directly to the public rather than via the traditional travel agencies. While this was highly commendable, traditions die hard and the necessary support was slow in materialising. Consequently after only a few weeks Air Atlantique was forced to conform and also reduce the number of daily sorties that its sole 748 G-BEKG made to Guernsey and Jersey. At the end of the summer season the services were subcontracted to National Commuter, but following a successful application from Jersey European to take over the routes, Air Atlantique ended its association with schedules. Subsequently JEA operated on the sectors alongside Air UK, albeit with reducing frequencies, until by 1994 the airline had dropped Southampton from its network.

Undoubtedly without the popular Channel Islands routes Southampton's scheduled traffic would be considerably reduced. Poor loads on the Birmingham sector were responsible for BA contracting its twice daily visit to Birmingham European in 1989, but after a year the route was suspended. On the credit side 1990 saw Capital introduce a link with Leeds using a SD3-60 until the carrier's demise, while JEA added Belfast City to its coverage for a time. Internationally the airport nowadays has services to Amsterdam, Brussels, Cherbourg and Paris, the latter route now sustaining three carriers. One of these is Manx Airlines which has established a hub at Southampton for a series of domestic and European schedules.

One of the more popular features of the airport for the travelling public is the close proximity of Parkway railway station. Many passengers use the economical rail-air ticket facility from London to the Channel Islands, the through journey taking about three hours.

With the demolition of the elderly decaying hangars early in 1989, the area was converted into a temporary car park with the original, more distant site relegated to serve as an overflow. It was the start of a major redevelopment project with Stage One including a new terminal complex north of the existing buildings. It was designed as a low structure with a number of curves helping it to merge into its surroundings. All of the passenger handling procedures are carried out at ground level with a minimum of walking involved, while natural light is used wherever possible through large areas of glazed roof panels. When completed, Southampton possessed one of the most modern and attractive regional airport terminals which was three times bigger than its elderly predecessor. There are 14 stands provided, all able to handle aircraft of Boeing 757 dimensions, the largest type for which the airport is licensed. However, in reality most of the flights are undertaken by smaller capacity machines such as the Jetstream 41, Friendship, BAe 146 and an occasional Boeing 737. In addition to the terminal, a number of other facilities have been redeveloped including the fire station, control tower, hangars and a cargo complex. Some £21 million has been invested in the airport, the only major element left unchanged being the runway, since its length is adequate for all traffic likely to be accommodated. For the same reason there are no plans for a second strip. Following these impressive improvements, Southampton has been able to record a significant increase in traffic figures as more carriers add the airport to their route network.

Location and access: Situated 4 miles north-northwest of the city off A355 at M27 Junction 5. There is a combined short- and long-term car park for 1,500 vehicles (600 and 900 respectively). Buses pass the airport entrance on their way to and from the city but are not particularly frequent. Trains to Parkway station from Southampton Central take 7min, whereas from Waterloo the journey time is about 60min. The station is well under 100m from the terminal

Terminal: A spacious new building containing waiting and refreshment area landside, with similar facilities for airside passengers

Spectator facilities: Unusually the designers recognised the need for a dedicated area for those wishing to wave at departing passengers, or to generally observe the movements. An admission-free, high-level internal balcony has therefore been provided in the terminal which gives excellent views over the apron. Access is via a long flight of stairs within the building. Although south facing, it is possible to obtain reasonable photographs through the tinted glass. Alternatively ground level shots are possible through the fence separating the car park from the apron

Operators: Scheduled services by Air UK (Friendship, Fokker 100), Aurigny Air Services (Trislander), Brit Air (ATR42, SAAB SF340), Brymon Airways (Dash Eight), European Airways (Jetstream 31), KLM (SAAB SF340), Manx (BAe ATP, Jetstream 41). *Charter and IT operators:* Air Europa (Boeing 737), Aurigny Air Services (Short SD3-60), British Airways (BAe ATP), Palmair Flightline (BAe 146)

Movements (1994): Total 57,876 (air transport 23,314/positioning 1,289/test & training 5,835/club 14,166/private 12,702). Total passengers 483,723

Runway: 02/20 (5,653ft/1,723m)

Radio frequencies: 118.2MHz (Tower)/128.85MHz (Approach)

Telephone: Eastleigh (01703) 629600

Operated by: Airports (Southampton) UK Ltd

SOUTHEND (ROCHFORD)

Flying first took place on the site in 1915, a year or so after it had been earmarked for the use of the Royal Flying Corps. For most of the war it became the home of squadrons involved in home defence, but once peace was restored Rochford was quickly returned to farmland. So it remained for over 10 years, until in 1933 Southend Corporation acquired the land in order to build an airport. Although it was September 1935 before it officially gained this status, civil flying had begun some time earlier following the creation of a local club. With the opening of the facilities, the Essex terminal of an existing ferry service to Rochester was moved to the new base, while the same year saw a Clacton-Southend-Margate operation started.

Quickly requisitioned in September 1939, all civil flying ceased and the airfield took the name of RAF Rochford for use as a satellite for Hornchurch. Various fighter squadrons spent short periods at this forward base for defence purposes before and during the Battle of Britian. In 1941 offensive fighter sweeps were

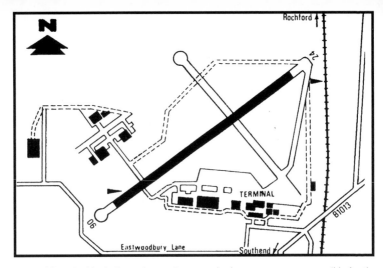

mounted from Rochford, the station coming under the control of North Weald in the spring of the following year. Back with Hornchurch in 1943, Spitfires and Mustangs stayed for short periods, but already the peak activity had passed. An Armament Practice Camp was established at the airfield in February 1944, the resident Masters and Martinets dragging drogues about the sky for the benefit of the temporary visitors. With the departure of the unit, Rochford spent a short time on a care and maintenance basis, but was reactivated as a satellite for Hornchurch in September 1944. This was to be the final change because at the end of 1945 it was closed by the Air Ministry prior to derequisitioning during the next year.

East Anglian Flying Services moved into the newly reopened airport, at first engaging in charter and pleasure flying, but by 1950 scheduled services had begun. Steadily the company grew in size, its network expanding to provide Southend with links to many destinations. Renamed Channel Airways in October 1962, the airline became the largest of those based at the airport. It therefore was a serious blow when the carrier collapsed in 1972, but fortunately other companies ensured that operations continued, abeit not on the same scale. Aviation Traders had set up an engineering facility at Southend in 1949, most of the work at first involving the maintenance of aircraft used on the Berlin Airlift. When this ended the company remained at Southend, subsequently becoming one of the largest organisations in the UK. Apart from its Carvair

work, the company was responsible for the rejuvenation of the Tudors in the 1950s, a scheme to convert ex-RAF Prentices for civilian owners and the design and construction of the Accountant Airliner.

In addition to IT charters by the locally-based airlines, Southend also became a busy centre of cross-Channel car ferry operations in the 1950s. Freighters were used initially, but later the locally-built Carvair took over with great success. In the face of considerable competition from the new roll-on/roll-off ships, British Air Ferries gradually ran down this type of service until by the mid-1970s they had ended. Instead the airline concentrated on passenger operations, both scheduled and charter, using Heralds. However, a further change of policy in late 1978 saw a transfer of route licences to British Island Airways, BAF reverting to purely charter and leasing activities.

After its official launch in January 1980, Air UK continued to use the Heralds leased from BAF on the services based at Southend. However, these were run down gradually both in frequency and the number of destinations on offer. In 1981 the airline formed its Air UK Commuter Services network equipped with Bandeirantes. The intention was to use the smaller aircraft on those routes with traffic of lower density. Southend qualified on this basis and although only Amsterdam, Rotterdam and Ostend were served, improvements to the timings were made to cater particularly for businessmen. Despite this effort the scheme was not particularly successful, resulting in Air UK removing its presence from Southend at the end of the 1983 summer season.

Meanwhile, a change of owner had given BAF the opportunity to expand into the scheduled market once again. Rapidly it became a busy operator, providing regular flights to the Channel Islands from an increasing number of points in the UK. In addition to possessing the largest fleet of Viscounts in the world, BAF also employed Heralds, Short SD3-30s and SD3-60s all of which used the airport for maintenance checks and overhauls at the company's engineering facility.

Unfortunately, towards the end of 1987 the airline began to run into financial difficulties. Although it continued to operate freight and passenger charters, all scheduled activities were ended while a new owner was sought. Eventually the company was merged with Baltic Airlines which had been established as a Viscount operator for a short time. The restructured BAF continued to concentrate on its charter contracts with Viscounts and Heralds until in the summer of 1990 it began operating the first of two One-Elevens.

Undoubtedly Southend's scheduled traffic figures received a set-back with the loss of BAF's contribution, but the airport still had a few regular services available. Maersk Air linked it with Billund in Denmark using Dash Sevens and Friendships at first, but later its new Fokker 50s were introduced on the twice-daily run. Even before the BAF cutbacks, 1987 has seen the suspension of the Rotterdam service by Holland Aero Lines. Never a particularly profitable route, the move really reflected the experiences of carriers through the years.

Fortunately, there are usually newcomers willing to try again and in this case Regionair took over the Dutch sector with a Bandeirante. In the meantime locally-based National Airways had been steadily developing its charter activities, but in mid-1987 it entered the scheduled scene as National Commuter with a regular service to Brussels in conjunction with SABENA. This was followed by others to Paris and the Channel Islands while licences were obtained for various European routes, but before any further expansion was possible, the airline and its network were taken over by Regionair in late 1989. Barely six months later the latter was itself forced to cease trading due to the familiar shortage of money, but in this case a new owner was quickly found to allow a resumption of the company's activities on a reduced scale. It meant that the proposed re-equipment was shelved and the Bandeirante reinstated.

Runways had been laid in 1955, but obstructions outside the airport's boundary imposed restrictions. In order to attract the attentions of IT operators the authorities carried out extensive ground clearance work at the threshold of Runway 06 in 1981. By removing several cottages it enabled more economic loads to be flown from the airport without the need for actual runway extension. As a result several tour companies introduced Southend to their programmes with flights to such destinations as Tenerife, Malaga and Palma. It encouraged further improvements this time with the reconstruction and modernisation of the terminal in 1986. General improvements, to the runway and taxiways were completed during the next couple of years or so, in order to attract even more IT traffic.

Despite this effort there was no dramatic increase in the degree of interest displayed. Southend-based Burstin Travel had endured much inconvenience due to the unreliability and general indifference of its contracted carriers, so it decided to launch its own airline to overcome this handicap which hitherto had given a poor impression to its clients. Accordingly, in the spring of 1990, Princess Air began an impressive programme of IT flights, both from its home base and other UK airports. A BAe 146-200QC had been chosen so that a high rate of utilisation could be maintained by using the machine for night cargo work, but the limit imposed on the number of night flights permitted restricted the growth of this type of business.

After many years of uncertainty, Southend was finally sold by the Council in 1994, the new owners being Regional Airports Ltd. The latter promptly gave a boost to the airport's future prospects by renaming it London Southend, followed by the announcement of the first phase of a £1 million redevelopment programme in 1995. One of the early items to receive the contractor's attention was the terminal building, which quickly lost its front section. This part of the structure had been added to the original many years ago when expansion was needed to ease the constant congestion. With this situation now a memory, more compact but modern accommodation is adequate for the small number of commercial flights using the airport. Elsewhere on the site, many of the individual sheds were earmarked for demolition, with the occupants rehoused in other buildings such as the refurbished Viscount House.

Scheduled services returned for the 1995 summer season, although only to the Channel Islands on Saturdays, Sundays and Wednesdays by either Aurigny, Titan or BAC Express. There are hopes that IT operators may be persuaded once again to use the facility in the future. With the demise of Princess Air, National and Regionair several years ago, Southend lost its resident charter and scheduled operators, although British World is still very much in evidence. However, it uses the airport for its maintenance activities rather than operational flying these days, much of which is carried out from Stansted and other regional centres.

Location and access: Situated 2 miles north of Southend, off the A127. Car park free.
A Southend Corporation bus serves the airport from the Central bus station with a journey time of about 10 min
Terminal: Contains lounge area with very good buffet which produces hot snacks in addition to sandwiches and cakes. The windows in this area overlook the apron
Spectator facilities: None provided. There are good views from the large windows in the lounge area of the terminal adjacent to the check-in. Photography is possible through the glass above the sticky finger level. Vantage points exist in the car park alongside the light

aviation area. Photographs can also be obtained from this point. Good landing shots can be taken at the threshold of Runway 06 in Eastwoodbury Lane when the wind is from the northeast
Operators: Seasonal scheduled services by Aurigny Air Services (Short SD3-60), BAC Express (Short SD3-60) and Titan Airways (ATR42). *Charter and IT operator:* Air Malta (Boeing 737). *Cargo and mail flights:* Willow Air (Trislander, Bandeirante and Short SD3-30)
A considerable number of movements are made by club, private and company aircraft, both UK and foreign registered, when using the airport as a gateway into or out of the country
Movements (1994): Total 51,223 (air transport 3,138/positioning 1,720/test & training 2,452/club 32,229/private 10,514). Total passengers 834
Runway: 06/24(5,265ft/1,605m)
Radio frequencies: 127.725MHz (Tower)/128.95MHz (Approach)
Telephone: Southend (01702) 340201
Operated by: Regional Airports Ltd

STANSTED

The airfield was built for and by the US forces in World War 2, work starting in August 1942. Known as Station 169, from August 1943 the base became responsible for the handling of damaged aircraft and maintaining the supply of replacements to operational groups. On 9 February 1944 the 344th Bomb Group moved in equipped with B-26 Marauders. Many

of the operations flown from Stansted were in support of the invasion of France and the subsequent advances. The Group transferred to a continental base in September 1944, leaving the airfield to return to its role of a tactical Air Depot.

After the war the RAF took over, setting up 263 MU on the base, whose task it was to

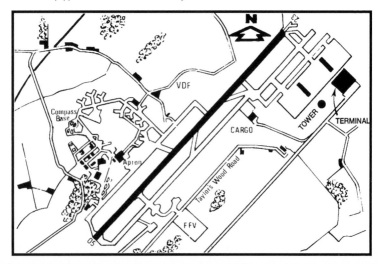

dispose of the vast quantities of surplus stores. By December 1946 it was possible for a civilian operator to join the dwindling RAF personnel, the Halifax sorties of London Aero and Motor Services launching Stansted as a cargo centre. Despite the initial success, LAMS was wound up in July 1948, leaving the smaller but active Kearsley Airways to maintain charters with Dakotas from the airfield, until it too ceased commercial flying two years later. In this case it was a voluntary decision, the company preferring to continue in an engineering role as it has to the present day. The Ministry of Civil Aviation assumed control of Stansted in 1949, moving their flying unit from Gatwick soon afterwards. It has remained ever since.

In the 1950s several carriers flew long distance charters especially on Government contracts, while considerable airfield development was undertaken by the Americans with a view to using it as a strategic base. The resultant 10,000ft runway certainly enhanced its future as an airport.

The 1960s found Stansted developing once again as a major freight centre with both Lloyd International and Transmeridian building up their businesses with Britannias and CL-44s. This activity continued until the collapse of British Cargo Airlines in March 1980 drastically reduced the amount of freight handled. It came at an unfortunate time since a brand-new cargo terminal had just been completed. Gradually, however, this type of traffic has picked up due to the locally based HeavyLift and Instone Air Line plus overseas carriers using Stansted on a regular basis.

Passenger traffic increased enormously with the arrival of Channel Airways who operated both schedules and ITs with Viscounts, One-Elevens, Tridents and Comets. In February 1972 once again Stansted witnessed the departure of its major residents when Channel ceased operations, followed soon afterwards by Lloyd.

During Channel's occupation, a brand-new terminal had been built, replacing the buildings erected for the 344th Bomb Group a quarter of a century earlier. The improvements attracted several foreign airlines engaged in charter work, but after a time the US carriers began to favour Gatwick. European companies continued to support the airport in varying degrees, the Scandinavian airlines proving the most consistent.

After the demise of Channel, scheduled services were restricted to a single seasonal Jersey flight by British Midland until 1 November 1978. Air Anglia then introduced a weekday service to Norwich and the north, which was greatly expanded in the summer of the following year.

A nominal change of carrier took place in January 1980 when Air UK was launched. The new airline continued the reduced winter timings on the Norwich route, a trend also noted during the following summer. The company found it necessary to suspend its Stansted operations completely at the end of 1980, eventually to return to introduce an Amsterdam link in November 1981. With slight adjustments, this service has continued to be included in the Air UK programme. Two other international licences were won in the early 1980s, namely Brussels and Paris. It was intended that initially they would form a Bandeirante network, the latter sector pending French approval. It was some time before either route was introduced; in fact the airline lost the Brussels licence to Jersey European, the company starting services in the spring of 1982.

This carrier had first served Stansted in 1980, when a schedule to the Channel Islands was launched. The frequencies offered were a marked improvement on those available for some years, although by 1982 the size of equipment had shrunk from Viscount/Herald to Bandeirante and later Twin Otter operations. Both of the latter types were also employed on the link between Stansted, Liverpool and Dublin, services which were inaugurated in December 1981. Poor results quickly brought an end to this route, a fate also suffered by that to the Belgian capital. Air UK applied to the CAA to take over the Brussels licence, this time starting up shortly after authority was received. Flown at first by Bandeirantes, increasing traffic soon justified larger aircraft. Further international routes have subsequently been added while approval has been received for several others. Competition came in April 1987 when Air France began a twice-daily schedule to Paris using SAAB 340As, but the timings did not affect the British company unduly. Similarly KLM joined it on the popular Amsterdam sector, although this time it was under a pool arrangement. However, by the start of the 1988 summer season the Dutch carrier realised it was more sensible for Air UK to resume responsibility for all Schiphol flights. Domestic services were not overlooked by Air UK, as requests were made in 1987 for both Belfast and Glasgow to be added to the network so that the Stansted hub could be built up in readiness for the completion of London's third airport. Additionally the company, together with British & Commonwealth Holdings and the Viking International Group, announced the creation of a new carrier in June 1987 to operate ITs from its Stansted base. Known as Air UK (Leisure) Ltd, arrangements were made so that two leased Boeing 737-200s could begin flying for the airline in April 1988. In October the first 737-400 was delivered, the type chosen for the permanent fleet.

With Stansted's future secure at last, several new carriers were attracted to the airport, one such company being Highland Express. Equipped with a single Boeing 747, after much time in the planning stage the airline finally began operations at the beginning of June 1987, staging through Prestwick en route to New York several times per week. This venture was relatively short-lived, ending in December with the collapse of the carrier. London Express was another that hoped to begin commercial flying with a 747, the destinations proposed for its regular sorties all being in the Far East. Financial problems postponed the launch planned for the autumn of 1986, but the company was still confident that it would be able to start up some time in the future. Indeed in early 1988 preparations were under way for operations to begin in the summer by Swan Airlines, the successor to London Express. This also failed to materialise.

Thurston Aviation moved its activities to Stansted in 1978, at the same time offering a handling service for the operators of executive aircraft. The company later set up Tal-Air, a carrier which then became involved in the movement of small packets and parcels to the Brussels hub of Federal Express. This American freight airline began flying to Europe in 1985 employing specially modified Boeing 727s for the lengthy run from Memphis. It was not long before DC-10-30s were substituted, the type staging through the Essex airport on four days each week while en route to Brussels. A rejuvenated Tradewinds moved its operating base from Gatwick to join HeavyLift Cargo Airlines at Stansted in 1986, but on the debit side Instone moved out to Coventry.

Aviation Traders (ATEL) was established at the airport for many years, undertaking maintenance overhauls and conversions on a wide range of types, particularly Boeing 707s. Some years ago the company became a subsidiary of Aer Lingus, but in March 1987 ATEL was acquired by privately-owned Qualitair Group of Cambridge. In conjunction with the airport's expansion, the new owner built an engineering facility at the airport which was sufficiently large to enable it to take two Boeing 747s or up to 10 Boeing 737s. In September 1989 the company was acquired by the Swedish group, FFV Aerotech.

Stansted's future as London's third airport was the subject of many debates and inquiries, but the uncertainty ended when work finally started on its development in April 1986. Access roads and car parks were laid at remarkable speed, while the site for the proposed terminal was enthusiastically attacked by scrapers and similar earthmoving devices. Long-standing landmarks disappeared to make way for the new structures which began to take shape at an early stage. Meanwhile the contractors were busy with the rail spur from the main line just north of Stansted station. This involved a tunnel under the airport but the work was completed in 1989 in readiness for track laying and the erection of the overhead wires. When completed, trains equipped with new rolling stock linked the airport with London (Liverpool Street) at half-hourly intervals. The terminal was designed to present a spacious appearance with all passenger activity on one floor level. International travellers are transported to and from the aircraft via a tracked transit link to a satellite building containing the departure lounge and airbridges. Domestic passengers are obliged to walk to the second satellite which opened in 1994, using a lengthy footbridge from the main terminal. Its presence tends to spoil the futuristic design of the building and gives the impression of being an afterthought by the creator, who in fact received an award for his efforts.

Location and access: Situated off the A120 three miles from Bishop's Stortford with direct access from M11 Junction 8. Both short- and long-term car parks are available with charges graduated to NCP standards. Regular trains run to and from Liverpool Street at 30min intervals with a journey time of 40min. Local buses operate between the airport and Bishop's Stortford, while Eastern National runs services to a range of towns in the area. Cambridge Coach Services connect Stansted with Cambridge, Heathrow and Gatwick, together with High Wycombe and Oxford. Greenline and National Express also provide links with northern and central England plus London (Victoria) at regular intervals

Terminal: Ramps, escalators and lifts give passengers direct access from the BR station, car park and coach stands to the single floor allocated for the usual processing arrangements. It also contains refreshment facilities, shops and bank

Spectator facilities: None provided. Those viewing can use the paved area adjacent to the terminal, but is too distant for anything other than vaguely waving at a departing shape. It is therefore necessary to locate a few suitable vantage spots around the perimeter. Photographs are not easy to obtain nowadays and are mostly confined to landing shots away from the inquisitive gaze of the security forces. Generally, the airport is probably one of the worst of its kind in the UK, if not Europe, for the lack of facilities for visitors

Operators: Scheduled services by Air Exel (Brasilia), Air UK (BAe 146, Fokker 50, Fokker 100, Friendship), Aviaco (DC-9), CSA Czech Airlines (Boeing 737), Cubana (DC-10), El Al (Boeing 747/757/767), Finnair (DC-10, MD11), Gill Airways (ATR42/72), Jersey European Airways (BAe 146), Luxair (Brasilia, Fokker 50), Manx Airlines (Jetstream 41), Ryanair (Boeing 737), Ryanair UK (Boeing 737), Proteus (Beech 1900), Tarom (Boeing 737, One-Eleven), Turkish Airlines (Airbus A310). *Charter and IT operators:* Aeroflot (Tu-134/154, Il-62), Air Bristol (One-Eleven), Air Europa (Boeing 737), Airtours International (Airbus A320, Boeing 757), Air Transat (Boeing 757, TriStar), Air 2000 (Boeing 757), All Leisure (Airbus A320), Air Malta (Boeing 737), Air VIA (Tu-154B), Aviaco (DC-9, MD88), Britannia Airways (Boeing 757), British Midland (Boeing 737), British World Airlines (BAe 146, One-Eleven), Cyprus Turkish Airlines (Airbus A310), European Aviation Air Charter

(One-Eleven), Finnair (DC-9, MD83), Futura (Boeing 737), Istanbul Airlines (Boeing 737), Leisure International (Airbus A320, Boeing 767), Maersk Air (Boeing 737), Oasis (MD83), Onur Air (Airbus A300/A320/A321), Premiair (Airbus A320, DC-10), Sunway (MD83), Titan Airways (ATR42, BAe 146, Short SD3-60), Transwede (Fokker 100, MD80). *Cargo flights:* Aeroflot (Il-76), Air Sofia (An-12), Balkan (An-12), British World Airlines (Viscount), Business Air (SAAB SF340), Channel Express (Electra, Herald), DHL (Boeing 727, DC-8), Emerald Airways (HS 748), Emery Worldwide (DC-8), Federal Express (DC-10, MD11), HeavyLift (An-12, Belfast, Boeing 747, Il-76), Martinair (Boeing 747, MD11), Polar Air Cargo (Boeing 747), South African Airways (Airbus A300, Boeing 747), Titan Airways (ATR42, BAe 146, Short SD3-60), TNT (BAe 146), Turkish Airlines (Boeing 727), VolgaDnepr (An-124)

Movements (1994): 75,261 (air transport 57,670/positioning 6,699/test & training 2,835/private 7,753). Total passengers 3,288,544
Runway: 05/23 (10,000ft/3,048m)
Radio frequencies: 123.8MHz (Tower)/125.55MHz, 126.95MHz (Approach)
Telephone: Bishop's Stortford (01279) 680500
Operated by: Stansted Airport Ltd

TEESSIDE (MIDDLETON ST GEORGE)

The airport's early days followed a familiar pattern since it was built as an RAF station. Taking the name of Middleton St George, its first resident was the Whitley V-equipped No 78 Squadron which arrived on 10 April 1941, staying some seven months. It returned for a further short spell in 1942, this time using Halifax IIIs. It meant that Middleton now had two Halifax units as No 76 Squadron had been at the base since 1941. During the course of its many operations, it had in fact become the first unit to drop the 8,000lb bomb, an event which occurred on 10/11 April 1942 during a raid on Essen.

By October 1942, both founder members had departed, the vacant airfield quickly receiving Nos 419 and 420 Squadrons, RCAF, the latter being replaced by another Canadian Squadron, No 428, in June 1943. The two units remained at Middleton until the end of the war, exchanging their Halifaxes for Lancaster Xs for the last year of operational service in the UK.

After the war, the airfield was earmarked for

development as a fighter base. However, it was used as a training establishment for some years, housing 13 OTU, 2 ANS and 205 AFS at various times. Operational life began again in February 1957 when Nos 92 and 264 Squadrons arrived using Hunter F6s and Meteor NF14s respectively. Middleton was without aircraft for a period in 1957/8 to allow a considerable modernisation programme to be completed. The Hunters of No 92 Squadron returned but in the meantime No 264 had exchanged the Meteors for the later Javelin and had become No 33 Squadron, subsequently remaining at Middleton until its eventual disbandment in November 1962. Its companion No 92 Squadron, became Fighter Command's official aerobatic team known as the Blue Diamonds, leaving the base in May 1961.

The supersonic age arrived in June 1962 when the Lightning conversion Squadron was formed with the first two-seater Mk 4s. It was renamed 226 OCU on 1 June 1963, soon afterwards adding some Mk 1s to its inventory.

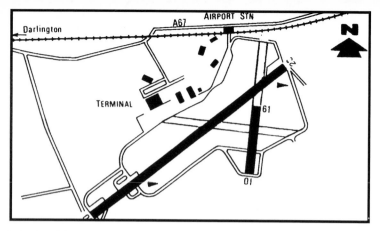

In October of that year it was announced that the RAF was vacating the airfield, mainly on grounds of economy. The OCU moved out on 13 April 1964, with Middleton passing to the local authorities for the sum of £340,000.

Now known as Teesside, civil flying commenced on 1 October with the first scheduled service two weeks later to Manchester. BKS soon added others including routes to Amsterdam, Belfast, Dublin, Düsseldorf and London.

Toward the end of 1966 BKS withdrew its operations, Autair acquiring the London licence. The airline used Heralds on the route with Luton as the southern terminal, which was later changed to Heathrow. Teesside became one of the halts for the imaginative bus-stop service started by Channel Airways in January 1969. It was then possible to travel northwards to Aberdeen via Newcastle and Edinburgh, or south to Stansted via Leeds and East Midlands with connections available to other airports such as Southend and Norwich. It unfortunately lasted only ten months, the airport losing a very useful facility.

At this time Autair dropped out of the scheduled scene, the London service being taken over by British Midland which has held the licence to the present day. Air Anglia began its use of the airport in 1972, adding it as an intermediate stop on the Norwich-Aberdeen route, a service continued by its successor, Air UK. The new airline soon began to prune its network, however, one of the casualties being the Glasgow link which was transferred to the locally-based Casair Aviation. This company continued to operate Navajos, expanding its Teesside network in 1982 to include Gatwick

and Belfast on weekdays. For this purpose a Short SD3-30 was acquired, further employment being found for it when a couple of seasonal weekend services were reintroduced to Guernsey and the Isle of Man. In the autumn of 1982 the carrier merged with Eastern and Genair, operations continuing under the latter name until its demise in 1984. Casair subsequently resumed flying under its original title, taking over the Glasgow and Humberside sectors from the licence holder, Air Ecosse, but in March 1988 the company once again ceased its activities.

Although Dan-Air maintained a token presence until its demise in 1992, its contribution was only a transit stop by a BAe 146 on the Newcastle-Amsterdam service. Attempts to provide new routes have been made by several small companies, but few have been successful. Travellers on scheduled services do not therefore have a great deal of choice, but at least they can still reach Heathrow or Amsterdam for onward connections. Similarly the airport is not over-endowed with IT flights, although the number has risen in recent years.

Location and access: Situated on the A67, six miles east of Darlington. Direction signs can easily be followed from the A1(M) and A66(M) to the airport. Car park has graduated charges. A regular bus service from Darlington Feethams runs every 30min taking 25min for the journey. Trains from Middlesbrough stop at the airport station every 30min with a journey time of 20min. From Stockton the service is hourly, journey time being 20min. A coach connects the station with the airport terminal
Terminal: Comprises modern single-storey

buildings, containing a buffet, restaurant, bar, shop and lounge area, while the original officers' mess nearby has been converted into the well-equipped St George Hotel

Spectator facilities: A roof terrace is provided from where viewing is generally satisfactory. As a photographic vantage point it poses problems due to it being set back from the front of the building. In any event, on bright days conditions are more favourable in the afternoons

Operators: Air UK (Fokker 50, Friendship), British Midland (Fokker 100). *Charter and IT operators:* Air Europa (Boeing 737), Air Kilroe (Jetstream 31), Air Malta (Boeing 737), Airtours International (Boeing 757), Airworld (Airbus A320), Britannia Airways (Boeing 757)

Movements (1994): 55,311 (air transport 14,498/test & training 2,075/club 33,011/private 3,677). Total passengers 408,552

Runways: 05/23 (7,516ft/2,291m), 01/19 (2,428ft/740m)

Radio frequencies: 119.8MHz (Tower)/118.85MHz (Approach)/128.85MHz (Radar)

Telephone: Darlington (01325) 332811

Operated by: Teesside International Airport Ltd

WICK

Wick was opened as a grass airfield in 1935, receiving the scheduled services of Aberdeen Airways and Highland Airways. Operations continued until 1939, although the latter company had by this time become a part of Scottish Airways. At the outbreak of war the airfield was taken over by the Air Ministry, becoming an important base for both Fighter and Coastal Command squadrons operating over the North Sea and Scandinavia. It also saw BOAC Mosquitos engaged on the Swedish diplomatic service when they called for refuelling.

Airline services were expanded after the war, this time from a much larger and better equipped airfield. Both Scottish and Allied Airways served Wick in the immediate postwar period, but the operations were soon taken over by BEA.

The routes never proved a very profitable part of the airline's network, especially when eventually it was necessary to employ Viscounts on the services. British Airways began to withdraw some of the short stage Highland and Island routes including some from Wick in 1976. Loganair took over the responsibility for these links, initially using Islanders and Trislanders, although the latter type was replaced by Twin Otters after a time.

Until the early 1980s, British Airways continued to ply a couple of routes to Aberdeen and the Shetlands using BAe 748s and

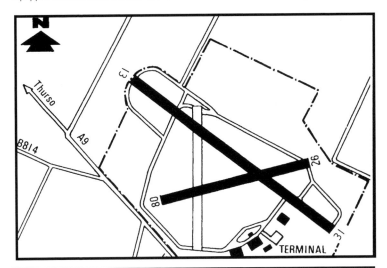

Viscounts, but eventually the airline pulled out of Wick. The airport gained the services of Air Ecosse, a comparative newcomer to the scheduled scene. It took over the Aberdeen licence, also adding Sumburgh and the Faroe Islands to its expanding network using Twin Otters and Bandeirantes. Varying fortunes created the need for several reorganisations within this airline, until finally in early 1987 financial problems forced it to suspend operations. Peregrine had been operating some of the services for Air Ecosse, but at this point there was a general scramble for the licences held by the latter. Leading these applications was British Airways which wanted to win back the Aberdeen-Wick route, a wish granted by the CAA. Strong protests were made by Air Ecosse at the loss of what was one of the company's most lucrative sectors. It was especially important because attempts were being made to attract a new owner, but it was not until late 1988 that the carrier was taken over by Peregrine. By 1990 BA had found that Wick still did not generate a great deal of traffic on the Edinburgh sector, so in the absence of a small-capacity type, the airline subcontracted the operation to Peregrine, resulting in the reintroduction of Bandeirantes and Gulfstream 1s to the twice-daily, Mondays to Fridays, schedules until the demise of the company. In the present day the same three routes are flown from Wick with the Aberdeen sector operated by Gill Airways' Short SD3-30s, while Loganair in its British Airways franchisee guise offers regular SD3-60 flights to Edinburgh. The latter type and Islanders are used for the scheduled run to and from Kirkwall.

Occasional visits are made by executive and light aircraft in connection with North Sea oil work or the nearby atomic power plant at Dounreay.

Location and access: Signposted off A9 in town of Wick. Situated on outskirts. Car park free
Terminal: Small single-storey building containing lounge. Buffet facility
Spectator facilities: Good viewing from vicinity of terminal. Photographic opportunities good using a standard or telephoto lens
Operators: Scheduled services by Loganair (Short SD3-60, Islander), Gill Airways (Short SD3-30)
Movements (1994): Total 6,007 (air transport 3,661/positioning 396/test & training 380/club 1,423). Total passengers 38,139
Runways: 08/26 (3,399ft/1,036m), 13/31 (5,297ft/1,609m)
Radio frequency: 119.7MHz (Tower)
Telephone: Wick (01995) 602215
Operated by: Highlands and Islands Airports Ltd

Below:
Through the years the grass area allocated to spectators at Blackpool has gradually shrunk until it finally disappeared in favour of the new terminal building. However, it is still possible to obtain the occasional photograph from the west side of the complex, as shown by the JEA Short SD3-60 G-OBHD.
A. S. Wright

Top:
The Air 2000 Airbus A320 G-OOAC seen landing on Bristol's Runway 27. *A. S. Wright*

Above:
The larger types using Terminal 3 at Heathrow often taxi by within range of a camera lens, or alternatively are towed from the maintenance area, as in the case of Qantas Boeing 747-400 VH-OJH. *AJW*

Top:
Photographs from the terminal at London City can only be taken when airside, although take-off shots are possible from the long-term car park. At present SABENA leases Dash Eights from Schreiner Airways for its Brussels schedule but this may change with the delivery of RJ85s. *AJW*

Above:
Luton handles many bizjet movements, this example being Falcon 50 VR-BKG. *AJW*

AIRFIELDS GUIDE

In this section brief notes are given of location and use of airfields not covered earlier, including those serving the northern islands and Alderney with scheduled operations. Excluded are the vast majority of private airstrips.

Aberporth (Dyfed) North side of A487, 5 miles northeast of Cardigan

Alconbury (Cambs) Near junction of A14 and A1, 4 miles northwest of Huntingdon, USAF

Alderney (Channel Isles) Southwest of island, 1 mile from St Anne. Civil. Aurigny services to south coast and France. TWR 125.35MHz

Andover (Hants) West of town, south of A303. AAC Helicopters. Middle Wallop satellite

Andrewsfield (Essex) Between Gt Dunmow and Braintree to north of A120 towards Saling and Stebbing. Civil. Light aircraft. A/G 130.55MHz

Audley End (Essex) One mile west of Saffron Walden off A130. Civil. Light aircraft. A/G 122.35MHz

Badminton (Avon) Six miles east-northeast of Chipping Sodbury off B4040. Civil. Light aircraft. A/G 123.175MHz

Barra (Western Isles) On foreshore of Traigh Mhor. Civil. Loganair services, air-taxi operations. A/G 130.65MHz

Barrow/Walney Island (Cumbria) Two miles northwest of town at north end of island. Civil. Operated by Vickers Ltd. Executive aircraft. TWR 123.2MHz

Barton (Greater Manchester) Five miles west of Manchester to north side of A57 and 1 mile west of M62 Junction 2. Civil. Light aircraft. A/G 122.7MHz

Battersea (London) South bank of Thames west of Battersea Bridge off A3205. Westland Heliport. Civil and military helicopters. TWR 122.9MHz

Beccles (Suffolk) Two miles southeast of town on north side of B1127. Civil. British International Helicopters. A/G 134.6MHz

Benbecula (Western Isles) Northwest side of island north of B892. Civil. British Airways services. TWR 119.2MHz

Benson (Oxon) Ten miles southeast of Oxford, 1 mile northeast of Wallingford by A4074. RAF, Queen's Flight aircraft. No 60 Sqn Wessex, London & Oxford UAS Bulldogs. APP 122.1MHz

Bicester (Oxon) Two miles northeast of town on east side of A421. RAF Gliding and Soaring Association. Light aircraft

Biggin Hill (Kent) East side of A233, 4 miles north of Westerham. Civil. Light and executive aircraft. APP 129.4MHz. TWR 134.8MHz

Binbrook (Lincs) Ten miles southwest of Grimsby north of B1203. Global Aviation

Birkdale Sands (Merseyside) South of Southport, west of A565. Civil seasonal pleasure flying with light aircraft and helicopters

Blackbushe (Hants) Four miles west of Camberley on north side of A30. Civil. Light and company aircraft. A/G 122.3MHz

Bodmin (Cornwall) To south of A30, 2 miles northeast of Bodmin. Civil. Light aircraft. A/G 122.7MHz

Booker/Wycombe Air Park (Bucks) Three miles southwest of High Wycombe, east of B482. Civil. Light aircraft. Personal Plane Services. A/G 126.55MHz

Boscombe Down (Wilts) Five miles north of Salisbury, east of A345 south of A303 at Amesbury. MoD, A & AEE. Empire Test Pilots School. Test and research aircraft, Southampton UAS

Bourn (Cambs) Seven miles west of Cambridge on south side to A428. Civil. Light aircraft, helicopters, crop sprayers. A/G 129.8MHz

Brawdy (Dyfed) Nine miles northwest of Haverford, west north of A487. No 202 Sqn B Flt SAR helicopters

Brize Norton (Oxon) Five miles southwest of Witney, west of A4095 east of B4020. RAF No 10 Sqn VC-10s, No 101 Sqn VC10 tankers, No 216 Sqn TriStar

Brough (Humberside) Six miles west of Hull, 2 miles south of A63. British Aerospace works Blackburn F/C & Humberside Police F/C. TWR 130.55MHz

Bruntingthorpe (Leics) Six miles south of Leicester off A50. Aviation Museum

Catterick (Yorks) East of A1, south of town. RAF. Firefighting training school, 645 VGS Grob Viking

Chalgrove (Oxon) Eight miles southeast of Oxford on north side of B480. Civil. Martin Baker Ltd.

Challock (Kent) Three miles west of village south of A252. Civil. Light aircraft. Kent Gliding Club, 618 VGS

Chester (Cheshire) See Hawarden

Chetwynd (Shropshire) Three miles north of Newport, east of A41. RAF. RLG for Shawbury

Chirk (Clwyd) East of A5, 1 mile north of village, 5 miles east of Llangollen. Civil. Light aircraft. Restorations

Chivenor (Devon) Four miles west of Barnstaple, south of A361. RAF No 22 Sqn A Flt SAR helicopters

Church Fenton (Yorks) Six miles northwest of Selby, southwest of B1223, north of B1222. RAF RLG for Linton. York UAS/9 AEF Bulldogs. TWR/APP 126.5MHz

Clacton (Essex) West of town near holiday camp. Civil seasonal pleasure flying. A/G 122.325MHz

Coltishall (Norfolk) Nine miles north of Norwich to west of B1150. RAF Nos 6, 41 and 54 Sqns Jaguars

Compton Abbas (Dorset) East of minor road to Blandford Forum, 2 miles south of B3081, 2 miles east of Shaftesbury. 800ft hill involved. Civil. Light aircraft. A/G 122.7MHz

Coningsby (Lincs) One mile south of A153 west of B1192, 15 miles northeast of Sleaford. RAF Tornado F3 OCU/56 Sqn, Nos 5 and 29 Sqn

Cosford (Shropshire) Nine miles northwest of Wolverhampton, west of A41, northwest of Albrighton. RAF Technical Training. Birmingham UAS Bulldogs. Aerospace museum TWR 122.1MHz

Cottesmore (Leics) Four miles northeast of Oakham north of B668. RAF. TTTE Tornado base

Cranfield (Beds) Four miles east of M1 between Junctions 13 and 14 north of A421. Civil. Cranfield University. Cessna agent. TWR 123.2 MHz, APP 122.85MHz

Cranwell (Lincs) Four miles northwest of Sleaford to north of A17 and astride B1429. RAF College No 3 FTS. Tucano, Red Arrows Hawks

Crosland Moor (Yorks) Three miles southwest of Huddersfield off A62. Civil. Light aircraft. A/G 122.2MHz

Crowland (Lincs) Six miles south of Spalding off A1073. Civil. Light aircraft A/G 130.1MHz

Culdrose (Cornwall) One mile southeast of Helston, east of A3083. RN helicopters, Jetstreams. TWR 122.1MHz, APP 134.05MHz

Cumbernauld (Strathclyde Reg) Six miles west-southwest of Falkirk, north of A80. Civil. Light aircraft. TWR 120.6MHz

Denham (Bucks) From A40 west of A412, 1 mile north of A40 and M40 Junction 1. Civil. Light aircraft. A/G 130.725MHz

Dishforth (Yorks) Four miles east of Ripon on east side of A1. RAF. RLG for Linton. AAC helicopters. Gliders. TWR 122.1MHz, APP 129.15MHz

Dornoch (Highland Reg) South of town on A949 east of A9. Civil. Light aircraft

Dounreay (Highland Reg) Eight miles west of Thurso, north of A836. Civil. Executive and light aircraft. Serves atomic power station. TWR/APP 122.4MHz

Dunkeswell (Devon) Five miles northwest of Honiton, west of minor road off A30 to Hemyock. Civil. Light aircraft. A/G 123.475MHz

Dunsfold (Surrey) Nine miles south of Guildford west of A281, south of B2130, east of village. British Aerospace plant. TWR 124.325MHz

Duxford (Cambs) Nine miles south of Cambridge, 8 miles east of Royston on south side of A505. M11 Junction 10 adjacent. Civil. Historic Aviation Centre. IWM, Duxford Aviation Society etc. A/G 122.075MHz

Earls Colne (Essex) Five miles southeast of Halstead off A604. Civil. Light aircraft. A/G 122.425MHz

East Fortune (Lothian) South of B1377, 3 miles north of East Linton and A1. Civil. Light aircraft. Museum of Flight

Eday (Orkney) West of B9063, centre of island. Civil. Loganair services

Eglinton (N. Ireland) Seven miles north of Londonderry on A2. Civil. Light aircraft. Loganair and Jersey European schedules with SD3-60s

Elstree (Herts) West from A5183 on to A411 in village for short distance before right on minor road. Civil. Light and executive aircraft. A/G 122.4MHz

Enniskillen (N. Ireland) Five miles north of town off A32. Civil. Light aircraft. A/G 123.2MHz

Enstone (Oxon) Five miles southeast of Chipping Norton north of A34, east of B4022, 1 mile from village. Civil. Light aircraft. A/G 129.875MHz

Fairford (Glos) North of Swindon, 4 miles west of Lechlade, south of A417. USAF 9 RW U-2R. Reserve base

Fair Isle (Shetland Isles) Centre of island. Civil. Loganair services

Fairoaks (Surrey) Three miles north of Woking to south of A319. Civil. Executive and light aircraft . A/G 123.425MHz

Farnborough (Hants) West of A325, north of A323. MOD.Corporate aircraft

Fearn (Highland Reg) Ten miles northeast of Invergordon (Cromarty Firth) south to B9166. Civil. Light aircraft

Felthorpe (Norfolk) Eight miles northwest of Norwich, south of village and west of minor road north of A1067, 2 miles east of Attlebridge. Civil. Light aircraft

Fenland (Lincs) South of minor road, 1 mile west of B1168, 5 miles south of A151 at Holbeach. Civil. Light aircraft. Fenland Aero Club. A/G 122.925MHz

Fetlar (Shetland) Centre of island. Civil. Loganair services

Filton/Bristol (Avon) Four miles north of city, west of a A38. British Aerospace. Test airfield. Rolls-Royce aircraft. Airbus components. TWR 132.35MHz, APP 122.72MHz

Finmere (Bucks) Three miles west of Buckingham, south of A421 (near junction with B4031). Civil. Light aircraft

Finningley (Yorks) Between A638 and A614 north of Bawtry and south of B1396, southeast of Doncaster. RAF No 6 FTS. Dominies, Jetstreams. No 100 Sqn Hawks. TWR 122.1MHz, APP 120.35MHz

Flotta (Orkney) Centre of island, west of B9045. Civil. Oil charter traffic. A/G 122.15MHz

Fordoun (Grampian Reg) South of B966, 1 mile west of A94, 9 miles southwest of Stonehaven. Civil. Light aircraft

Fowlmere (Cambs) Three miles northeast of Royston off A505. Civil. Light aircraft. A/G 120.925MHz

Gamston (Notts) West of B6387 north of A1, 3 miles south of Retford. Civil. Light aircraft. A/G 130.475MHz

Glenrothes (Fife Reg) Two miles southwest of town, east of B922, north of B921, west of A94. A/G 130.45MHz

Goodwood (Sussex) Off A285 north of Chichester. Civil. Light aircraft. TWR 120.65MHz, APP 122.45MHz

Gt Yarmouth/North Denes (Norfolk) On west side of A149, 2 miles north of Gt Yarmouth. Civil. Light aircraft. Pleasure flying. North Sea oil traffic. TWR 123.4MHz

Halfpenny Green (Staffs) Five miles east of Bridgnorth, southwest of Wolverhampton off B4176. Civil. Light aircraft. A/G 123.0MHz

Halton (Bucks) Three miles southeast of Aylesbury, north of A4011, south of B4544. RAF Technical Training. A/G 130.425MHz

Haverfordwest (Dyfed) East of A40, 2 miles north of town. Civil. Light and executive aircraft. A/G 122.2MHz

Hawarden (Cheshire) Four miles west-southwest of Chester, north of A55. British Aerospace/Airbus production. TWR 124.95MHz. APP 123.35MHz

Headcorn (Kent) Southeast of village, east of A274, about 9 miles southeast of Maidstone. Civil. Light aircraft. Crop sprayers. Lashenden Air Warfare Museum. Parachute School. A/G 122.0MHz

Henlow (Beds) East side of A600 at junction with A6001, 2 miles southeast of Shefford. RAF. Museum store

Henstridge (Somerset) South of A30, 2 miles east of A357. Civil. Light aircraft. A/G 130.25MHz

Hethel (Norfolk) Near East Carleton between A11 and B1113, 7 miles southwest of Norwich. Civil. Light aircraft. Lotus cars. A/G 122.35MHz

Honington (Suffolk) North of Bury St Edmunds between A143 and A1088, 5 miles south of Thetford. RAF

Hoy/Longhope (Orkney) Half mile southwest of Longhope. Civil. Loganair services

Hucknall (Notts) One mile southwest of Hucknall, south of B6009. Civil. Rolls-Royce. Light aircraft. A/G 130.8MHz

Islay/Port Ellen (Strathclyde Reg) South end of island, west of A846. Civil. Loganair services. TWR/APP 123.15MHz

Kidlington (Oxon) Six miles northwest of Oxford on north side of connecting road between A34 and A4260 from village. Civil. Oxford Air Training School. CSE. McAlpine Helicopters. TWR 118.875MHz, APP 125.325MHz

Kinloss (Grampian Reg) North side of B9089 just east of junction with B9011 off A96, 3 miles northeast of Forres. RAF Nos 120, 201, 206 Sqns Nimrods

Kirkwall (Orkney) Southeast of Kirkwall off A960. Civil. British Airways. Loganair schedules. Oil-related charters. TWR 118.3MHz

Lakenheath (Suffolk) Five miles north of Barton Mills west of A1065, east of B1112. USAAF No 48 FW F-15s

Lasham (Hants) Five miles south of Basingstoke to east of A339, 4 miles northwest of Alton. Civil. FFV maintenance base. Gliding centre

Leeming (Yorks) East side of A1 south of A684 to Northallerton. Nos 11 and 25 Sqns Tornados. Northumbrian UAS/11 AEF Bulldogs. TWR 122.1MHz, APP 127.75MHz

Lee-on-Solent (Hants) Four miles west of Gosport south of B3334, 3 miles south of Fareham. RN. HMS *Daedalus*. Helicopters. Communications aircraft. Civil. Light aircraft. Gliders. TWR 135.7MHz

Leicester (Leics) Four miles east-southeast of city east of B667, connecting road between A47 and A6 near Stoughton. Civil. Light aircraft. A/G 122.125MHz

Leuchars (Fife Reg) Seven miles southeast of Dundee on east side of A919. RAF Nos 43 and 111 Sqns, Tornados, No 22 Sqn B Flt, SAR helicopters, Aberdeen, Dundee & St Andrews UAS/12 AEF Bulldogs

Lindholme (Yorks) Six miles northeast of Doncaster on east side of A614, 3 miles south of A18. RAF. RLG for Finningley. Gliders

Linton-on-Ouse (Yorks) West of A19 at Shipton, 10 miles northwest of York. Minor roads via Newton-on-Ouse to airfield. RAF. No 1 FTS. Tucanos. No 642 VGS Vigilants. TWR 122.1MHz APP 129.15MHz

Little Gransden (Cambs) Five miles southeast of St Neots. Civil. Operated by Fordaire. A/G 130.85MHz

Little Snoring (Norfolk) Four miles northeast of Fakenham, 1 mile north of A148. Civil. Light aircraft

Little Staughton (Cambs) Four miles west of St Neots, west of B645 (old A45). Civil. Light aircraft

Lossiemouth (Grampian Reg) West of B9135 off A941, 5 miles north of Elgin. RAF Nos 12, 15 and 617 Sqns Tornados. No 16 Sqn Jaguars. TWR 118.9MHz, APP 119.35MHz

Lyneham (Wilts) South of A420, 8 miles southwest from M4 Junction 16. RAF Lyneham Transport Wing. Hercules. TWR 123.4MHz, APP 118.425MHz

Machrihanish/Campbeltown (Strathclyde Reg) Four miles west-northwest of Campbeltown, 2 miles west of A83. RAF. Used for exercises. Loganair services. APP 125.9MHz, TWR 122.1MHz

Marham (Norfolk) North of A1122 between Downham Market and Swaffham. RAF Nos 2 and 13 Sqns Tornados

Merryfield (Somerset) Between A358 and B3168 north of Ilminster. RN. Satellite for Yeovilton. Helicopters

Middle Wallop (Hants) Six miles southwest of Andover, southeast of A343 at junction with B3084. AAC. Helicopters and light aircraft. Museum of Army Flying. TWR 122.1MHz, APP 126.7MHz

Mildenhall (Suffolk) On south side of A1101, 3 miles from A11 at Barton Mills. USAF transports and tankers, USN aircraft. No 21 SOS MH-53J

Mona (Gwynedd) North side of A5, 9 miles west of Menai Bridge. RAF. Satellite for Valley. Light aircraft. APP 134.35MHz

Netheravon (Wilts) Six miles north of Amesbury, 2 miles east of A345. AAC. Helicopters. Civil. Light aircraft

Netherthorpe (Yorks) Two miles southwest from A57, 3 miles northwest of Worksop. Civil. Light aircraft. A/G 123.275MHz

Newbury (Berks) One mile east of town off A34. Light aircraft, helicopters race days only

Newmarket Heath (Cambs) West of A1304 (old A11), south end of town. Light aircraft race days only. A second strip used for July course. All landings on Runway 14, departures on 32

Newton (Notts) Eight miles east of Nottingham north of A52, south of minor road west of A46. RAF. E Midland UAS/7 AEF Bulldogs. TWR/APP 122.1MHz

Newtownards (N. Ireland) Off A20 southeast of town. Civil. Light aircraft. A/G 123.5MHz

Northolt (Greater London) North side of A40 west of junction with A4180, 2 miles east of Uxbridge. RAF. No 32 Sqn BAe 125, Gazelle. Civil executive visitors. TWR/APP 126.45MHz

North Ronaldsay (Orkney) Southwest side of island. Civil. Loganair services

North Weald (Essex) North side of B181 south of A414, 2 miles northeast of Epping. Essex Gliding Club. Tugs. Aces High, The Squadron, Harvard Team, light aircraft. A/G 123.525MHz

Nottingham/Tollerton (Notts) East of city, to south of A52 and north of Tollerton village. Civil. Light aircraft. A/G 122.8MHz

Oban/Connel North (Strathclyde Reg) West of A828, 5 miles northeast of Oban. Civil. Air taxi and light aircraft, microlights

Odiham (Hants) Eight miles north of Alton to east of B3349 (old A32), 2 miles south of M3 Junction 5. RAF Nos 7 Sqn Chinooks, 27 and 33 Sqns Puma

Old Sarum (Wilts) Two miles north of Salisbury to east of A345. Civil. Light aircraft. Gliders. A/G 123.2MHz

Old Warden (Beds) Two miles west of Biggleswade signposted off A1 opposite junction with A6001 from east. Civil. Light aircraft. Shuttleworth Collection. A/G 123.05MHz

Oronsay (Strathclyde Reg) South end of island. Civil. Loganair flights

Panshanger (Herts) Four miles west of Hertford, south of B1000, west side of link road to A414 at Cole Green. Civil. Light aircraft. A/G 120.25MHz

Papa Stour (Shetland) On south side of island. Civil. Loganair flights

Papa Westray (Orkney) On west side of island. Civil. Loganair services

Perranporth (Cornwall) Ten miles northwest of Truro west of the B3285, southwest of village. Civil. Light aircraft, gliding centre. A/G 119.75MHz

Perth/Scone (Tayside Reg) Four miles northeast of Perth, west of A94. Civil. Air Service Training aircraft. TWR 119.8MHz, APP 122.3MHz

Peterborough/Conington (Cambs) Eight miles south of Peterborough, south of B660, east of A1. Civil. Light and company aircraft. A/G 129.725MHz

Peterhead (Grampian Reg) North of A950, 3 miles west of Peterhead. Civil. Light and company aircraft. Oil-related charters. A/G 123.375MHz

Popham (Hants) North side of A30, 2 miles west of M3 Junction 8. Civil. Light aircraft. A/G 129.8MHz

Portland (Dorset) South of Weymouth, to east of A354. RN. Helicopters. APP 124.15MHz

Predannack (Cornwall) North of Lizard Point to west of A3083. RN. Satellite for Culdrose. Helicopters

Redhill (Surrey) Off minor road 2 miles south of A25, 1 mile east of town. Civil. Light aircraft. Bristow Helicopters. TWR 120.275MHz

Rochester (Kent) Two miles south of town to west of A229, just north of M2 Junction 3. Civil. Light aircraft. A/G 122.25MHZ

St Athan (S. Glamorgan)) Ten miles west of Barry to north of B4265. RAF MU. Wales UAS Bulldogs, No 634 VGS Vikings

Samlesbury (Lancs) Six miles east of Preston between A59 and A677. British Aerospace. No 631 VGS Vikings. TWR 130.35MHz, APP 124.45MHz

Sanday (Orkney) Centre of island. Civil. Loganair services

Sandown (Isle of Wight) Two miles west of town, north of A3056. Civil. Light aircraft. A/G 123.5MHz

Scampton (Lincs) Six miles north of Lincoln, west of A15. RAF

Sculthorpe (Norfolk) Four miles west of Fakenham, north of A148. USAAF reserve base

Seething (Norfolk) Ten miles southeast of Norwich, south of village, east of minor road to B1135, 2 miles northwest of Bungay on A143. Civil. Light aircraft. A/G 122.6MHz

Shawbury (Shropshire) West side of B5063, north of A53, 9 miles northeast of Shrewsbury. RAF. Air Traffic School, No 2 FTS Gazelles and Wessex, Bulldog MU. TWR/APP 122.1MHz

Sherburn (Yorks) Four miles east of A1, east of village, south of B1222. Civil. Light aircraft. A/G 122.6MHz

Shipham (Norfolk) On north side of minor road southeast from A1075, 1 mile northeast of village and 4 miles south of East Dereham. Civil. Light aircraft. A/G 119.55MHz

Shobdon (Heref & Worc) Ten miles west of Leominster, south of village and B4362. Civil. Light aircraft. A/G 123.5MHz

Sibson (Cambs) Eight miles west of Peterborough, west of A1 on east side of B671. Civil. Light aircraft. Parachute club. A/G 122.3MHz

Silverstone (Northants) Seven miles northeast of Brackley, to east of A43. Civil. Open on race days. Light aircraft, helicopters. A/G 121.075MHz

Sleap (Shropshire) Nine miles north of Shrewsbury south of Wem west from B5476. Civil. Light aircraft. A/G 122.45MHz

Stapleford (Essex) Five miles north of Romford, south of A113, west of junction with B175. Civil. Light and executive aircraft. A/G 122.8MHz

Stornoway (Hebrides) North of A866, 3 miles east of Stornoway. Civil. British Airways, Loganair services. TWR 123.5MHz

Strathallan (Tayside Reg) Three miles northwest of Auchterarder, to west of B8062. Civil. Light aircraft. Parachute club. A/G 129.9MHz

Stronsay (Orkney) Northwest end of island, north of B9062. Civil. Loganair services

Sturgate (Lincs) Five miles southeast of Gainsborough between A631 and B1241. Civil. Light aircraft. A/G 130.3MHz

Sumburgh (Shetland) Twenty miles from Lerwick at south end of main island. Civil. British Airways, Loganair scheduled services. Charters by British World ATR 72s. Bristow and British International helicopters base. Oil industry charter traffic. TWR 118.25MHz, APP 123.15MHz

Swansea/Fairwood Common (W. Glamorgan) Six miles west of Swansea on A4118. Civil. Club, private and company operated aircraft. Helicopters. TWR/APP 119.7MHz

Swanton Morley (Norfolk) four miles north-northeast of EastDereham, 1 mile west of B1147 in Mill Street. AAC helicopters, civil light aircraft. No 611 VGS Vikings. TWR/APP 123.5MHz

Swinderby (Lincs) East side of A46, 7 miles northeast of Newark. RAF

Sywell (Northants) Five miles northeast of Northampton, east of A43 to north of village. Civil. Light aircraft. A/G 122.7MHz

Tatenhill (Staffs) Six miles west of Burton upon Trent, 1 mile east of A515 south of B5234. Civil. Light and executive aircraft. Allied Breweries. A/G124.075MHz

Ternhill (Salop) Southwest side of A41 southeast of junction with A53, 3 miles southwest of Market Drayton. RAF. RLG for Shawbury. No 632 VGS Vigilants. TWR 124.15MHz

Thruxton (Hants) Six miles west of Andover, north of A303. Civil. Light aircraft, helicopters. A/G 130.45MHz

Thurleigh (Beds) Five miles north of Bedford, north of minor road towards B660, 2 miles east from A6 at Milton Ernest. Experimental and research aircraft. TWR 130.0MHz

Tingwall/Lerwick (Shetland) Five miles northwest of Lerwick, southwest of A971. Civil. Loganair services. A/G 122.6MHz

Tiree (Srathclyde) In centre of island, north of B8065. Civil. Loganair services. TWR 122.7MHz

Tollerton (Notts) See Nottingham

Topcliffe (Yorks) East side of A167, 2 miles north of A168, 3 miles southwest of Thirsk. RAF. RLG for Linton-on-Ouse. AAC helicopters. TWR 130.825MHz, APP 125.0MHz

Unst (Shetland) East of A968, 2 miles southeast of Baltasound. Civil. Loganair services. RAF communications aircraft. TWR/APP 130.35MHz

Upavon (Wilts) South side of A342, 2 miles east of junction with A345, 8 miles north of Amesbury. RAF. Gliders, helicopters, light aircraft. No 622 VGS Vikings

Valley (Gwynedd) Five miles southeast of Holyhead, 1 mile south of A5. RAF. No 4 FTS and CFS Hawks, No 22 Sqn C Flt, SAR helicopters. APP 134.35MHz

Waddington (Lincs) Five miles south of Lincoln between A607 and A15. RAF No 8 Sqn Sentry. Frequent visits by European air forces for exercises

Warton (Lancs) On south side of A584, 4 miles east of Lytham. British Aerospace factory. Jaguars. Tornados. TWR 130.0MHz, APP 124.45MHz

Wattisham (Suffolk) Nine miles northwest of Ipswich, north side of B1078 from A14 (old A45) at Needham Market. AAC Lynx and Gazelle. TWR 122.1MHz, APP 124.925MHz

Wellesbourne Mountford (Warwicks) South of B4086, 1 mile west of A429, 4 miles east of Stratford-upon-Avon. Civil. Light and company aircraft. A/G 124.025MHz

West Freugh (Dumfries) Five miles southeast of Stranraer, west side by junction of B7084 and B7077. MoD (PE) trials aircraft. Avionic systems testing. TWR 122.55MHz, APP 130.05MHz

Westray (Orkney) North end of island. Civil. Loganair services

Wethersfield (Essex) East of B1053, 7 miles north-northwest of Braintree. No 614 VGS Vikings. USAF reserve base

Weybridge (Surrey) East of A318 south of Weybridge. Helicopters. A/G 122.35MHz

Whalsay (Shetland) Northeast end of island. Civil. Loganair services

White Waltham (Berks) Three miles southwest of Maidenhead, 1 mile south from A4 and A404(M) junction. Civil. Light aircraft. TWR 122.6MHz

Wickenby (Lincs) East of minor road, 1 mile north of B1399, 10 miles northeast of Lincoln. Civil. Light aircraft. A/G 122.45MHz

Wittering (Northants) Three miles south of Stamford on west side of A1. RAF. Nos 1 Sqn and 20 Sqn/HOCU Harriers

Woodbridge (Suffolk) North side of minor road, 2 miles east of B1083, 2 miles south of A1152. AAC exercises. No aircraft based

Woodford (Greater Manchester) Three miles east of Wilmslow, south of A5102. British Aerospace. Avro RJ production. TWR 126.925MHz, APP 130.75MHz

Woodvale (Merseyside) Five miles south-southwest of Southport, west of A565. RAF. Liverpool and Manchester UAS/10 AEF Bulldogs. Civil. Light aircraft. TWR 119.75HMz, APP 121.0MHz

Wroughton (Wilts) West side of minor road south from B4005, 1 mile east of A4361, 3 miles south of Swindon. Science Museum Collection. RN. Helicopters

Wyburton (Lincs) Two miles west of Boston, north side of A1121 near junction with A52. Civil. Light aircraft

Wycombe Air Park See Booker

Yeovil (Somerset) One mile southwest of town, south of A3088. Westland factory. Helicopter production. TWR 125.4MHz, APP 130.8MHz

Yeovilton (Somerset) Two miles east of Ilchester on south side of B3151 south of A303. RN. Helicopters. Sea Harriers. FAA Museum, Concorde Hall.

Top:
Good landing shots can be obtained at Manchester.
AJW

Centre:
Jetstream 41 demonstrator G-JMAC visits the domestic terminal at Manchester.
AJW

Above:
KLM ERA has expanded its presence at Norwich and now bases two S-76s at the airport.
A. S. Wright

Top:
A grass viewing area is provided alongside the terminal at Norwich from where the occasional photograph can be obtained, especially of Air UK Fokker 50s and Friendships. *AJW*

Centre:
Reasonable shots can be taken through the windows overlooking the apron at Southend, the subject often being a Short SD3-30 resting after its normal nocturnal freight carrying activities. *AJW*

Above:
Landing shots are possible at Stansted as illustrated by the Airbus A310 TC-JYK of Kibris Turkish Airlines. *AJW*